ARCHAEOLOGY AND THE BIBLE

50 FASCINATING FINDS
THAT BRING THE BIBLE TO LIFE

ARCHAEOLOGY AND THE BIBLE

50 FASCINATING FINDS
THAT BRING THE BIBLE TO LIFE

Tom Meyer

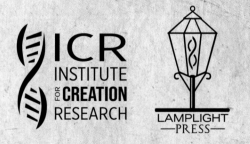

ICR
INSTITUTE
FOR CREATION
RESEARCH

LAMPLIGHT
PRESS

Dallas, Texas
ICR.org

Archaeology and the Bible

50 Fascinating Finds That Bring the Bible to Life

by Tom Meyer

First printing: June 2023

Unless otherwise specified, all Scripture quotations are from the King James Version.

ISBN: 978-1-946246-72-1
Library of Congress Catalog Number: 2023938811

Please visit our website for other books and resources: ICR.org

Printed in the United States of America.

Published by Lamplight Press, an imprint of ICR Publishing Group

Table of Contents

EXILE

Early Church Period

Introduction

During my undergraduate studies at Shasta Bible College in Redding, California, I went on a two-week trip to the Holy Land. It forever changed how I understand and appreciate the land of the Bible and the Word of God. As soon as I returned to America, I couldn't wait for the next time I could go back.

Upon finishing my B.A., I felt led by the Lord to return to Israel to pursue my higher education, as well as to participate in some very exciting missionary campaigns with Jews for Jesus. I ended up spending 1,000 days in the Holy Land earning two M.A. degrees at Jerusalem University College. I was the first student in the university's history to achieve such a feat.

From the professors in the classroom and the archaeological remains in the field studies, I was able to gain insights into the world of the Bible that are impossible to gain anywhere but where the events happened—the Holy Land. The more I learned about archaeology and the Bible, the more it confirmed what I already knew to be true, that "thy word is truth" (John 17:17).

We don't need archaeology to demonstrate that the Bible is true; it's the self-authenticating Word of God. But when I began to see how archaeology confirms the biblical record in every instance, I asked those in my inner circles and friends and family back home in America if they had ever heard of the objects I was learning about and how they demonstrate the reliability and accuracy of Scripture. Again and again the answer was "no."

I too had never heard of most of these objects, even with a B.A. in Bible and Theology, until someone taught me in Jerusalem. Even though I and those close to me had gone to church our entire lives, we were totally incapable of defending our faith using biblical archaeology—that is, until I became equipped and began to teach that indeed the stones do cry out (Luke 19:40).

That, in short, is the aim of this book—not only to praise God that His Word is truth, as wonderfully demonstrated by archaeology, but to equip you, your kids, and your grandkids with the truths you need to defend the faith. So, grab your fedora, your leather jacket, a water jug, and your Bible, and let's embark on an exciting journey to the Holy Land.

PATRIARCHAL PERIOD

1 Egyptian Execration Texts

The First Mention of Jerusalem Outside the Bible

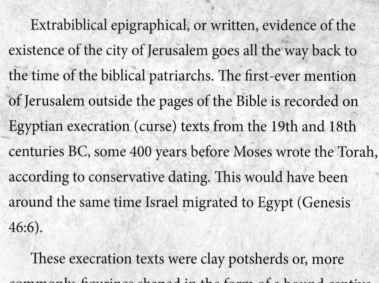

Extrabiblical epigraphical, or written, evidence of the existence of the city of Jerusalem goes all the way back to the time of the biblical patriarchs. The first-ever mention of Jerusalem outside the pages of the Bible is recorded on Egyptian execration (curse) texts from the 19th and 18th centuries BC, some 400 years before Moses wrote the Torah, according to conservative dating. This would have been around the same time Israel migrated to Egypt (Genesis 46:6).

These execration texts were clay potsherds or, more commonly, figurines shaped in the form of a bound captive and inscribed in Egyptian hieratic script with the different enemies and cities the pharaoh wanted to conquer with the help of the Egyptian gods. The figurines have been found buried at numerous places in Egypt, including the necropolis (cemetery) near the Great Pyramid at Giza and the necropolis near the famous Step Pyramid at Saccara.

Before the pharaoh would go out to battle, Egyptian magicians would perform a ceremony to ensure the

Egyptian execration figurine

The pyramids at Giza

Execration text on potsherds discovered in Giza

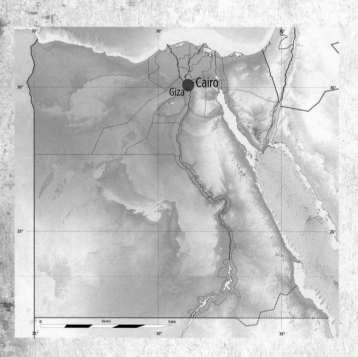

pharaoh's victory. According to a discovery that gives a partial record of the ritual, the clay figurines would be bound with rope and then humiliated through a series of shameful acts, like being spat on or burned. They were finally smashed to pieces and buried by the Egyptian priests, indicative of the desired fate awaiting the pharaoh's enemies.

Archaeologists discovered collections of such figurines that were used in a ceremony before one pharaoh's military campaign north into Canaan. Besides the city of Jerusalem, other biblical cities are mentioned, including Shechem, Hazor, and Ashkelon. The name of Jerusalem has been found in the 19th- and 18th-century BC collections on display in museums in Berlin and Brussels. These archaeological discoveries point to the geopolitical importance of Jerusalem at the time of the biblical patriarchs, which is in total accordance with the Bible's depiction of the significance of Jerusalem and its king, Melchizedek, at the time of Abraham in the 20th century BC (Genesis 14:18-20).

The archaeological discoveries of the Egyptian execration texts confirm that the places mentioned in the Bible are historically accurate.

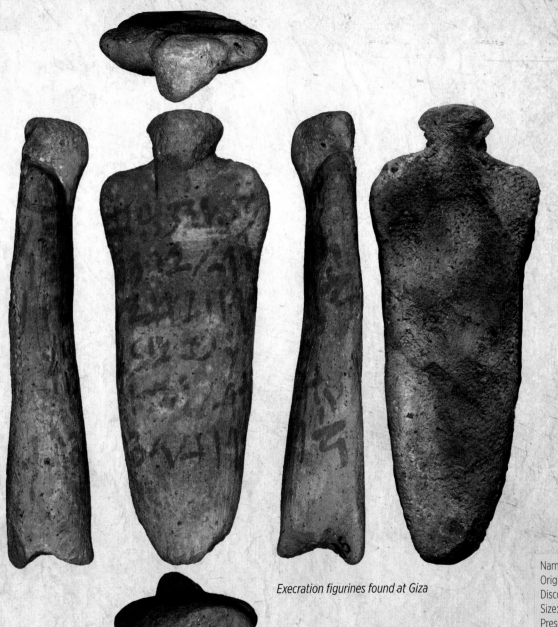

F 7465

Execration figurines found at Giza

Name: Egyptian execration texts
Origin and date: Egypt 19th and 18th c. BC
Discovered: numerous sites in Egypt
Size: varied
Present location: various museums

2 BENI HASAN MURAL

What the Patriarchs Might Have Looked Like

If you ever wondered what Abraham, Isaac, and Jacob might have looked like, thanks to archaeology you don't need to wonder anymore. In Egypt at the necropolis of Beni Hasan, located 150 miles south of Cairo on the eastern banks of the Nile River, a discovery helps illustrate what life was like in the Levant (Canaan) during the time of the biblical patriarchs.

The relatively unknown Beni Hasan mural was found by John Garstang of the University of Liverpool during a 1902 to 1904 excavation. A portrait was located on the wall of the rock-cut tomb of a high-ranking Egyptian official and vizier named Khnumhotep II, the son of a provincial governor. The picture dates to the sixth year of the reign of Pharaoh Sesostris II, about 1892 BC. This is important because the wall painting at Beni Hasan is somewhat concurrent with the biblical account of the Israelites who migrated to Egypt at the time of Jacob (Genesis 46:6).

The Beni Hasan tomb mural from the Middle Kingdom period of Egypt depicts, among other things, a caravan of Semitic people traveling from the Levant to pay homage

Beni Hasan mural

*View of the Nile River Valley
from the Beni Hasan cemetery*

Exterior of Beni Hasan ancient Egyptian cemetery

to an Egyptian ruler by bringing stibium, a cosmetic for painting the eyes. The mural portrays the travelers with a different skin color from the native African people shown. The yellow skin of those from the Levant was a standard Egyptian artistic style to differentiate Mediterranean-world foreigners from Egyptian people, who are normally depicted with red skin. The Nubians from south of Egypt are depicted with darker skin, along with other physical characteristics unique to their people group.

The mural provides an insight into the fashion, occupations, physical characteristics, etc. of people who lived in the Levant during the time of the biblical patriarchs. The colorful clothing of the people, their weapons, tools, instruments, and livestock are well documented. Even though the mural inside the rock-cut tomb at Beni Hasan wasn't specifically intended to portray the Israelites' migration to Egypt at the time of Jacob, it does show what their appearance might have been and the goods that might have accompanied the convoy of Israelites from Canaan to Egypt some 3,800 years ago.

Name: Beni Hasan tomb mural
Origin and date: Egypt ~1892 BC
Discovered: John Garstang ~1904
Present location: Middle Egypt

Illustration from the original mural, C. R. Lepsins, 1913

3 UR, ABRAHAM'S HOMETOWN

Even though Abraham lived over 4,000 years ago, windows into his past are still evident. For example, you can visit a well at Beersheba in Israel that he likely used and perhaps even owned. There's plenty of pottery at the bottom of this well from his time.

But even more spectacular evidence related to the biblical patriarch appeared in the 1920s, when significant finds were made in Abraham's hometown, the city of Ur in ancient Mesopotamia (Genesis 1:28-31). The perilous pathways to this location were no deterrent to tourists of the time. From all over the world, they flocked to Ur in southern Iraq, which was being excavated by the famous English archaeologist Sir Leonard Woolley. Even best-selling author Agatha Christie was agog at the treasures unearthed by the star archaeologist.

Perhaps Abraham didn't live within the city before departing for Canaan. He was a shepherd, after all, who would have mostly stayed out in the countryside. But Abraham would certainly have visited the metropolis of Ur for trading purposes. And what a metropolis it was. Woolley found the actual ancient temple where Abraham's contemporaries could have worshiped the moon god Nannar, sometimes called Sin. He discovered treasures like the golden vessels of Queen Puabi and Prince Mes-Kalam-Dug. Only Howard

Standard of Ur "War" panel, 26th century BC

Carter's discovery of King Tut's tomb in Egypt in 1922 garnered more attention in the mainstream media at the time.

In the tombs of Ur, Woolley also found fluted dishes, silver ornaments, chariot parts, ornate harps, a golden goat's head, and other artifacts. Metallurgy was commonplace at the time, as was writing. Within the city limits of Abraham's time (about 2000 BC), Woolley discovered one of the largest schools ever found in ancient Mesopotamia.

Countless clay tablets had been discarded by the students there.

Skeptics once considered Ur a myth and thought Abraham, if he even lived, would have been an illiterate shepherd. Instead, Ur was a prosperous city with a sophisticated culture, and Abraham was an educated man, as his successful business ventures show. Archaeology once again confirms that the places recorded in the Bible really existed.

City of Ur ruins in southern Iraq

4   DAN CITY GATE

Archaeological evidence has been unearthed that could relate to one of the most prominent people in the Bible—Abraham. The scarcity of archaeological evidence connected directly to him shouldn't be a surprise since the Bible depicts him as a seminomadic, tent-dwelling shepherd. Abraham didn't live in a house with foundations but traveled to different parts of Canaan during different times of the year around 4,000 years ago, according to conservative biblical chronology.

In comparison, consider that there's scant archaeological evidence that Napoleon and his army traveled from Egypt through the Holy Land in 1799. They, like Abraham, lived in tents. The only reason we can know with certainty that Napoleon and his army were present in the Holy Land is that the written record of Napoleon's historians testifies to the fact.

So, the harmony between the archaeological evidence and the Genesis 14 account of Abraham coming to the city of Dan to rescue his nephew Lot should come as no surprise. Excavations at Tel Dan by the Israel Department of Antiquities began in 1966. Archaeologists discovered a massive earth rampart

Name: Tel Dan arched gate
Origin and date: Canaan ~1750 BC
Discovered: 1979
Present location: Northern Israel

Bronze Age gate at Tel Dan. A wooden frame was installed at the entrance to allow interior excavation of the mudbrick arches.

Tel Dan archaeological site, Israel

around the ancient city that would have required about 800,000 tons of earth and rocks, equivalent to 40,000 semi-trailer loads.

The most amazing feature of this defensive structure is the triple-arched gate discovered at the southeast corner of the rampart. Abraham might have entered it when he rescued Lot. The gate is built of mudbrick, with stone steps approaching it. It stands 23 feet high and consists of two towers. About 50 courses of mudbrick are preserved, and the remains of almost 4,000-year-old lime and plaster still cling to the joints between the layers. Examination of the broken pieces of pottery found in the composition of the mudbricks, as well as potsherds found on the steps and on the floor of the gate itself, conclusively date the gate to the time of Abraham.

For an unknown reason, the gate wasn't used very long. The passageway and chambers were filled with compacted earth, and the entire structure was buried and another gate built on top of it. That decision preserved the ancient gate for the world to visit today. One can walk on the same stone steps and through the same gate that Abraham likely did some 4,000 years ago.

Steel frame showing the size and location of the temple altar at Tel Dan

Tel Dan Israelite gate

CANAAN CONQUEST AND JUDGES

5 BALAAM INSCRIPTION

Archaeological evidence has been found that demonstrates the historicity of the infamous biblical character Balaam, a soothsayer who lived in Mesopotamia. Balak, the king of Moab, hired him to curse the Israelites, who had invaded Balak's territory around 1400 BC on their way to Canaan. Balaam is probably best remembered, though, for the biblical account of his donkey speaking to him in a human voice after he beat her. She stopped because she could see the angel of the Lord blocking their way, though Balaam couldn't. So, the Lord enabled the donkey to speak and then opened Balaam's eyes so he could see the angel of the Lord (Numbers 22:22-31). Unsuccessful in his attempts to curse Israel, Balaam became synonymous with rebellion and apostate religion in later Jewish history (Revelation 2:14).

Some 600 years after Balaam lived, he posthumously retained his fame and following. In fact, he probably became more popular after he died. In 1967, archaeologists found a non-Hebrew temple from between 840 and 760 BC during an excavation in Deir 'Alla in modern-day Jordan. Inside the temple, archaeologists discovered a jigsaw puzzle of a find next to collapsed plaster walls. The fragmented plaster remains were eventually reconstructed to reveal an inscription that once decorated the temple walls.

The discovery, which some believe to be the oldest example of Aramaic literature in the world, was dedicated to none other than the "seer of the gods, Balaam, son of Beor." It's possible this pagan temple was a sort of school of prophets that began in the tradition of Balaam's prophecies, similar to the way prophets like Elijah and Samuel developed a following during the period of the Old Testament.

The temple linked to Balaam continued to function until the building was destroyed by an earthquake around the eighth century BC. The inscription was perhaps a way to commemorate one of Balaam's famous extrabiblical prophecies. In the inscription, he curses the gods who brought famine and death, and also petitions the fertility gods who could restore life and order to the region.

The Balaam inscription is one of over 100 examples in which archaeologists have found the name of a person mentioned in the Bible on an object buried in the earth. These discoveries demonstrate that such people were historical people, even notorious characters like Balaam the diviner.

Name: Deir 'Alla Inscription
Origin and date: Deir 'Alla ~880 BC
Discovered: 1967
Present location: Jordan Archaeological Museum

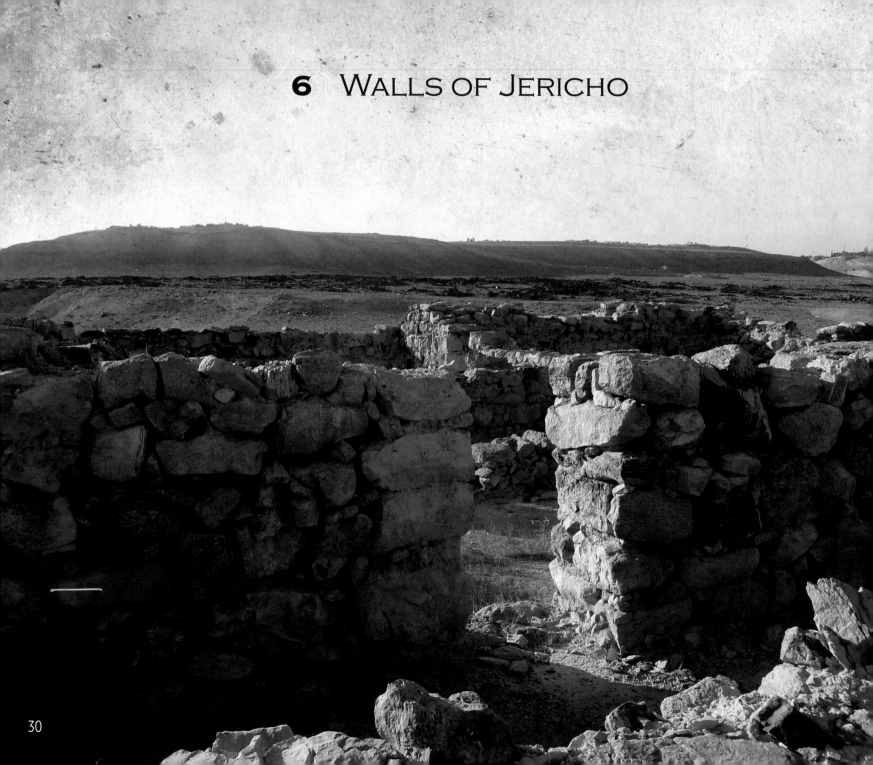

6 WALLS OF JERICHO

Though comparatively small by modern standards, Jericho was a heavily fortified ancient Canaanite city. It was essential for the Israelites to destroy it after they crossed the Jordan River in order for them to advance into Canaan. The fall of Jericho in approximately 1400 BC is an excellent example of textual and archaeological evidence corroborating each other.

According to the Bible, after marching around the walls of Jericho in silence for six days, the Israelites were to circle the city seven times on the seventh day. At the end of the seventh pass around the city, the priests were to blow the trumpets, and the people were to shout. God promised that when they did this, the walls would fall down flat (Joshua 6:4-5). The order of events was that the walls fell down, then the city was burned, and finally it was abandoned (Joshua 6:20-26).

Every archaeologist who has excavated Jericho has come to the same conclusion. A mudbrick wall once stood upon the stone retaining wall from the time of Joshua, parts of which can still be seen. According to the archaeologists, the mudbrick wall down to its base fell outward. Those who dug at the bottom of the stone retaining wall

The Walls of Jericho Fall Down, Gustave Dore

Name: Jericho walls
Origin and date: Jericho 1400 BC
Discovered: 1868 first excavations
Present location: West Bank, Palestine

found a pile of collapsed reddish mudbricks along the entire portion they unearthed. A diagram of the fallen mudbricks can be found in the excavation reports of British archaeologist Kathleen Kenyon.

Jericho is the only place where archaeologists have found a city wall that has completely fallen down. The fallen wall formed a ramp for the Israelite soldiers to go up into the city to take it. Archaeologists also found evidence of a massive destruction by fire from the same time period. In the three-foot-thick burn layer, they found room after room of ash, collapsed roof timbers, and large burned storage jars that were full of grain. This is significant because not only did Joshua command the soldiers not to raid the fallen city, but the Bible states that the Israelites invaded Canaan at harvest time (Joshua 3:15). The absence of structures on the layers of earth on top of the ash layer shows that the city was abandoned for an extended period of time.

Every archaeologist's report shows the walls collapsed first, then the city was set on fire, and subsequently the city was abandoned, just like the Bible states.

33

7 RAHAB'S HOUSE

A once-in-a-lifetime archaeological discovery demonstrates the historical reliability of the amazing account of Rahab, whose family members were the lone Canaanite survivors of the famous battle of Jericho (Joshua 6:25). Instead of attacking the southern frontier of Canaan, which was filled with walled cities and fortresses defending against attacks from Egypt, Joshua skirted around the southern fortifications and broke through the eastern front. This was poorly defended except for the region around Jericho. From there, Joshua could divide and conquer the southern and northern regions of Canaan, but it was essential to conquer Jericho first.

According to the Bible, Joshua first sent two spies to Jericho (Joshua 2:1). After arriving in the walled city, the Israelite spies inconspicuously entered the house of Rahab for cover. Seeing the writing on the wall of an imminent Israelite invasion, Rahab helped the spies. She hid them among stalks of flax laid out on her roof (Joshua 2:6).

Rahab knew the divine name of YHWH, what He had done to pharaoh's army, and His promises regarding Israel's land inheritance (Joshua 2:9-11). Because of their shared faith in YHWH, Rahab arranged with the spies to spare her house when the day came for the destruction of Jericho. The sign or token that would keep her home from harm was a scarlet cord hanging from the window. Sending the spies on their way, she hung the scarlet cord from the window right away, not knowing what fateful day her house would be passed over (Joshua 2:21).

Mudbrick walls at Jericho

35

Joshua Spares Rahab by Gustave Dore

According to the Bible, the miracle of the walls of Jericho collapsing happened shortly thereafter. In the three-foot-thick burn layer of Jericho dating to around 1400 BC (according to conservative dating), archaeologists John Garstang and later Kathleen Kenyon found room after room of ash, collapsed roof timbers, and large burned storage jars that were full of grain. This validates the biblical account of Jericho's fall in precise detail.

But the preservation of Rahab's family was part of the miracle, since their home was located on the city wall that came tumbling down. During excavations at Jericho from 1907 to 1909, German archaeologists Ernst Sellin and Carl Watzinger discovered on the northern side of Jericho a small portion of the lower city wall from the time of Joshua that did not tumble down, as the excavations unequivocally demonstrated happened everywhere else. According to the German team, the standing section of the mudbrick wall was about eight feet high, and the house built against it was also intact. Based on the biblical account, this portion of the wall and the adjacent house could be connected to Rahab.

Rahab the Canaanite assimilated into Israel and eventually became the great-great-great-grandmother of King David and the ancestor of Joseph, the husband of Mary, the mother of Jesus (Matthew 1:5-16).

8   THE TABERNACLE AT SHILOH

Archaeological clues have come to light that can help us identify the exact spot where the God of Israel tabernacled, or dwelled, among His people. The city of Shiloh, located in the heart of the biblical hill country, became the first capital of Israel shortly after the conquest of Canaan around 1400 BC (Joshua 18:1). The city was the cultural, religious, and political center of the new nation. Therefore, it was here that Israel pitched the tabernacle and here the Ark of the Covenant was placed.

According to the Talmud, the tabernacle stood in Shiloh for 369 years, from the time of Joshua until the death of Eli the high priest when the Ark of the Covenant was captured by the Philistines (1 Samuel 4). The Philistines were inflicted with disease, so after seven months they sent the Ark back to Israel (1 Samuel 6).

The tabernacle was a transitory structure that could be set up and taken down like a large tent, so we shouldn't expect to find any evidence of its foundations at Shiloh. For a modern-day parallel, there isn't any archaeological evidence that Napoleon and his army marched through Israel over 200 years ago, primarily because they camped in tents.

But archaeological clues have emerged that can pinpoint where the tabernacle once stood. Near the summit of Shiloh on the northern side is a rectangular area that's exposed to bedrock. This area,

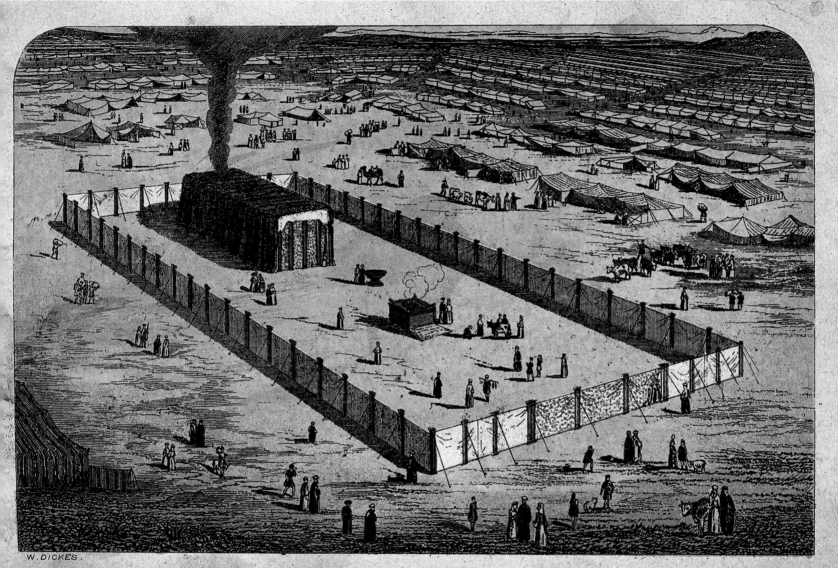

THE TABERNACLE IN THE WILDERNESS.

W. DICKES.

Horned altar reconstruction

known as the Tabernacle Plateau, is large enough to house the 150-by-75-foot tabernacle courtyard. Archaeologists found small cavities hewn into the bedrock of the plateau at intervals. These were perhaps postholes used to support the wooden poles of the outer tabernacle fence. Nearby, archaeologists discovered three stone horns that evidently once adorned three of the four corners of the horned altar in the courtyard (Exodus 27:1-2).

Also, a trove of animal bones was discovered nearby in the strata that date from the time of the tabernacle. The bones were overwhelmingly kosher and were likely the sacred remains of the sacrifices eaten by the priests. In fact, most of the bones came from the right side of the animals, which the Bible designated as the priest's portion of the sacrifice (Leviticus 7:32-34).

These clues fit together perfectly like pieces of a jigsaw puzzle, giving us confidence that we can pinpoint the exact spot where the God of Israel tabernacled among His people in the formative stages of Israel becoming a nation some 3,400 years ago.

Location of the remains showing where the tabernacle stood at Shiloh

9 THE AMARNA TABLETS

An Insight into Canaan at the Conquest

A treasure trove of ancient Egyptian tablets from the time of Akhenaten, the most infamous of the Egyptian pharaohs, has shed light on the happenings of the time. These tablets not only contain fascinating insights on the geopolitics of the Levant shortly after Israel's conquest of Canaan, but perhaps also provide extrabiblical information about the Hebrews at the time of the biblical judges.

Akhenaten was the 10th pharaoh of the 18th dynasty of the New Kingdom in Egypt. Originally named Amenhotep IV, the pharaoh changed his name in his early years to honor the god Aten. Akhenaten was educated at Memphis like most of the elite, then was established as pharaoh at Karnak. Akhenaten reigned over Egypt from approximately 1353 to 1336 BC. He defied the Egyptian establishment by replacing the chief deity of Egypt, Amun Re, with the lesser-known sun god Aten, and by building a new capital city devoted to the exclusive worship of Aten.

In 1887, local Egyptians illegally excavated the Place of Pharaoh's Correspondence at the ruins of Tell el-Amarna, the site of Akhenaten's capital city, and discovered 382 clay tablets about the size of the palm of your hand, which have become known as the Amarna tablets. The tablets are diplomatic correspondence between the pharaoh and the political rulers in Babylon, Assyria, and the Levant during the 14th century BC.

They were written over a span of two decades and are composed in Akkadian, the lingua franca or international trade language of the day.

Name: Amarna tablets
Origin and date: Tell el-Amarna ~1360–1332 BC
Discovered: 1887
Size: height 4 to 5 inches
Present location: various museums

Not only are biblical cities like Hazor, Megiddo, Gezer, and Jerusalem prominently mentioned, but over 100 of the tablets from local Canaanite vassals complain to the pharaoh about a group of rebels and raiders in Canaan called Habiru. The local Canaanite kings informed the pharaoh that if he didn't intervene quickly, the whole of Canaan would be overrun by these people.

The Habiru are mentioned in different ancient Near Eastern sources over a wide span of time, from the 18th to the 12th centuries BC, and appear not to identify a specific ethnic group but a social one. It seems to be a nickname or label given to different ethnicities of seminomads in the Levant who were extremely problematic to the indigenous population. Some even suggest a linguistic connection between the term Habiru and Hebrew.

Whatever the case may be, it is certain that not all Habiru were Hebrew. However, it's possible that the Canaanite kings writing to Pharaoh Akhenaten lumped the Hebrews into this social group of raiders and rebels who were causing a political upheaval in Canaan during the time of the judges, an account with which the Bible is in total accord (Judges 1:19-36).

Akhenaten

Amarna tablets

43

10   Hazor Burn Layer

Undeniable archaeological evidence has been uncovered pertaining to the biblical account of Joshua's destruction of the city of Hazor. This ancient site is situated nine miles north of the Sea of Galilee and 15 miles southwest of Dan. The site is comprised of two distinct areas—the mound proper, covering 30 acres, and a large rectangular lower area of 170 acres.

Hazor was a well-established city centuries before the time of Joshua. It is first mentioned in the Egyptian execration texts from the 19th century BC. Along with Dan, it's also the only Canaanite city mentioned in the Mari documents of the 18th century BC. These were Akkadian-language tablets discovered in Mari, an ancient Semitic city-state located in what is now Syria. Hazor's importance reached its climax in the 14th century BC, as reflected in the Amarna tablets.

At the time of Joshua, Hazor was the head of the northern Canaanite king-doms, the key city the Israelites needed to destroy to maintain their foothold in Canaan. According to the Bible, Jabin, king of Hazor, gathered with many inde-pendent northern kings at the waters of Merom for a localized world war of sorts against Joshua (Joshua 11:1-5). But Jabin's confederacy was surprisingly defeated by Joshua's army. With momentum on their side, the Israelites overran Hazor and subsequently burned it with fire, as they had with Jericho (Joshua 11:10-11).

The archaeological evidence that would testify to the reliability of the biblical account of Hazor's defeat lay dormant for almost 3,300 years. From 1955 to 1958, Israeli archaeologist Yigael Yadin led excavations that discovered that both the

View from Tel Hazor, Northern Israel, of the panoramic landscape of countryside and the Galilee mountains in the Hula Valley

upper and lower cities of Hazor were destroyed by a violent conflagration, as the Bible records. A huge ash layer in the mound is dated to around the 14th century BC and is contemporaneous with the Israelite conquest of Canaan.

The wealth of the palace and the cultic items in the temples were not looted but buried in the destruction debris, similar to the treatment at Jericho. If that weren't enough, many of the Canaanite statues and cultic items show evidence of intentional mutilation, which coincides with the Bible's mandate for Israel to destroy every vestige of Canaanite worship lest they fall into the trap of their religious customs and go after other gods (Deuteronomy 12:1-4).

As is the case with the discoveries at Hazor, whenever the claims of the Bible can be tested, the Bible proves to be historically accurate.

Typical Israelite four-room house. The people would have lived on an upper floor.

Excavation at Hazor of a temple or palace

11 Eglon's Palace

A British archaeologist has likely discovered the palace of Eglon, king of Moab, who was assassinated by the Israelite judge Ehud. During the biblical period of the judges, around 1300 BC, King Eglon controlled the coveted Medeba Plateau in what is now modern-day Jordan. He used it as a launching pad to push west to rule over the villages in Israel near Jericho, as well as north and west of Jerusalem. Jericho was Eglon's home base for collecting supplies from the raids in the region.

Ehud was moved to act because this oppressive Moabite king was robbing the poor to feed the rich. Ehud was from the tribe of Benjamin and came from a long line of warriors. He personally led the convoy to deliver the tribute payable to King Eglon with the intention of assassinating the king. Ehud was left-handed (Judges 3:15). He cleverly hedged his bets that the king's guards would not pat him down on his right thigh where his weapon was hidden; a right-handed man would keep his weapon on his left thigh. Ehud succeeded in smuggling his sword into King Eglon's palace.

Special attention is given in the biblical account to the obesity of King Eglon (Judges 3:17). Being a fat ruler was a sign of wealth in the world of the Bible. After receiving the tribute, which was likely paid in foodstuffs, King Eglon sent away the delegation without incident.

But Ehud sent the rest of the Israelites away and returned to the king to offer a secret message. The king's bodyguards then left, so King Eglon and Ehud were alone in the cool roof chamber of the royal residence. Ehud took this opportunity to rid Israel of its oppressor and reached for the blade strapped to his unchecked right thigh. King Eglon's enormous belly swallowed up the entire blade of the 18-inch sword and even the hilt. Unable to recover the

Tell es-Sultan, also known as Tel Jericho

49

Tell es-Sultan, better known as Tel Jericho

weapon, Ehud left it in the king and quietly left, locking the doors behind him (Judges 3:20-23).

While excavating Jericho in 1933, British archaeologist John Garstang determined that he had uncovered the palace of King Eglon. The small but luxurious building measured around 40 by 48 feet and was constructed somewhere around 1300 BC, contemporaneous with Eglon. Inside the palace, Garstang uncovered expensive local and imported pottery, which helped the dating process. He also found a tantalizing clue: a very rare cuneiform tablet. Though the tablet doesn't mention King Eglon by name, it testifies that the owner of the palace was a high-ranking government official. No other structures were found near the palace dating to the same time period, which fits with the curse that Joshua about 100 years earlier had put on anyone rebuilding the city of Jericho (Joshua 6:26).

John Garstang's evidence of the discovery of King Eglon's palace strengthens confidence in the historical accuracy of the biblical record.

The Death of Eglon (Dalziels' Bible Gallery)

Jericho ruins

51

12 MERNEPTAH STELE
The First Mention of Israel Outside the Bible

Despite the Israelites living in Egypt for 430 years (Exodus 12:40), the word "Israel" is only specifically found on one archaeological artifact from ancient Egypt—the Merneptah Stele. This one mention has tremendous implications for proving the historical accuracy of the Bible.

This unique record of Israel comes from approximately 1208 BC during the reign of Merneptah, an otherwise obscure pharaoh, the son and successor to the famous Ramesses the Great. The events recorded on the stele are likely contemporaneous with the Trojan War and the biblical period of the judges. The majority of the over 10-foot-tall black granite slab is dedicated to Pharaoh Merneptah's successful military campaign in northern Africa against the Libyans and their allies, the Sea Peoples, which included the biblical Philistines. The last two lines of the stele memorialize a separate military campaign into the land of Canaan, which was later known as the land of Israel. Upon his return to Egypt, the triumphant Merneptah ordered a stele constructed to commemorate his military success.

The stele was found over 3,000 years later in 1896 by the famous English Egyptologist and archaeologist Flinders Petrie. It was located in Merneptah's tomb at Thebes, also called Luxor, the ancient Egyptian capital on the banks of the Nile River. The victory stele, which was

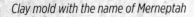
Clay mold with the name of Merneptah

originally placed in Merneptah's mortuary temple at Thebes, is now on display at the Egyptian Museum in Cairo.

This is, to date, the only time Israel is cited on any Egyptian artifact. Among the last lines of the stele, almost as a throwaway statement, the people of Israel are mentioned. After detailing how the pharaoh subdued the biblical cities of Ashkelon, Gaza, and Yanoam, which revolted against Egyptian rule, Merneptah brags that "Israel is desolate, its seed is no more."

The Egyptian expression associated with Israel here, "its seed is no more," signifies complete destruction or ruin of their people group. There's nothing in the Merneptah Stele's context to suggest that the destruction of agricultural products or grain is intended, as some scholars think. "Its seed is no more" was a formulaic phrase often used for defeated nations. Pharaohs tended to exaggerate their victories in their monuments.

Name: Merneptah Stele
Origin and date: Thebes/Luxor, Egypt ~1208 BC
Discovered: Flinders Petrie 1896
Size: height 10 feet
Present location: Egyptian Museum, Cairo

The Merneptah Stele in the Egyptian
Museum in Cairo, Egypt

Name of Israel in Egyptian hieroglyphs

Inside the Merneptah funeral chamber where the stele was found, there are wall reliefs that probably depict the pharaoh's battles. The battle scenes match the account engraved on the stele.

The Merneptah Stele is important for two reasons. First, this single Egyptian artifact mentioning Israel provides an extrabiblical source that the people of Israel were a bona fide people group living in Canaan around 1208 BC. Second, it helps eliminate Merneptah as a potential candidate for the pharaoh of the Exodus.

Again, archaeology affirms the historical accuracy of the Bible.

13 SAMSON THE STRONGMAN

Three archaeological objects have been unearthed that help us measure the historicity of the biblical strongman Samson. According to the Bible, Samson judged Israel during the "time of the judges," a period of 300 years before Israel had its first king (14th to 11th centuries BC, according to conservative dating).

One of these objects reflects the occasion when Samson encountered a lion and tore him apart with his bare hands (Judges 14:5-6). In 2012 archaeologists found a stone seal dating to the 12th century BC, perhaps contemporaneous with Samson. The seal depicts a strongman, presumably Samson, confronting a lion without a weapon in his hand.

The small seal, only 0.5 inch in diameter, was found at the city of Beth Shemesh. This was a hub city in the biblical lowlands that was within eyesight of Samson's home city of Zorah and a short walk from Timnath, the place where Samson slew the lion.

The second archaeological discovery supports the account of Samson killing Israel's enemies in one final feat of tremendous strength. According to the Bible, after Delilah cut Samson's hair, he was taken captive by the Philistines. When the rulers of the Philistines held a great festival to honor their god Dagon for capturing Samson, the blinded hero was brought from prison and ordered to entertain them.

Ruins at Tell Qasile, where an ancient Philistine temple was found

The temple where they celebrated was filled to capacity, with an overflow of 3,000 guests on the roof. Rocking furiously back and forth between the cedar pillars supporting the roof, Samson broke the pillars. The roof then collapsed, killing Samson and all the Philistines present (Judges 16:21-30).

Archaeological excavations from 1971 to 1974 at Tell Qasile, a Philistine city located in what is now northern Tell Aviv, uncovered extensive Philistine remnants. These included the foundations of a temple dating to about the 12th century BC, with two interior limestone pillar bases on which two cedar pillars supporting the roof had originally rested. The pillars were spaced just far enough apart that a strongman shifting his weight could collapse them both. It's uncertain if the temple at Tell Qasile is the actual temple Samson brought down, but every Philistine temple excavated in Israel has a similar architectural plan, showing the accurate rendering of the Samson account.

Lastly, in 2012 archaeologists digging in the city of Huqoq near the Sea of Galilee uncovered a synagogue from the fifth century AD. The exposed mosaic floor depicted two incredible scenes from the life of Samson. The first is the account of Samson catching 300 foxes, tying their tails together with a cord, then fastening lit torches to the cords and setting the foxes loose to destroy the entire spring crop of the Philistines (Judges 15:4-5). The other mosaic depicts Samson carrying the gates of Gaza to a hill near the biblical city of Hebron (Judges 16:3).

In every instance where the archaeological findings relate to the biblical account of Samson, the evidence confirms the Bible's record.

The Death of Samson, Gustave Dore

Huqoq mosaic inscription and face

14 MEDINET HABU RELIEF
What the Philistines Looked Like

Archaeological evidence from ancient Egypt provides clues to what one of Israel's greatest enemies, the Philistines, looked like.

The great Pharaoh Ramesses III commissioned wall reliefs to be constructed at his mortuary temple of Medinet Habu to commemorate his greatest achievements. The most popular account among the local Egyptian population was that of their great leader repelling the Sea Peoples' attempted invasion of Egypt by land and sea in the early part of the 12th century BC. The Philistines were one of several groups that made up the Sea Peoples.

The other side of the story might be that the Sea Peoples weren't trying to militarily invade Egypt but were instead forced to migrate from their islands because of a natural catastrophe and were only looking for a place to settle with their families on the eastern Mediterranean seaboard. Either way, the 3,200-year-old reliefs located on the northern outside wall of the temple were originally intended for propaganda and political purposes. They demonstrated the pharaoh's strength in defending the

borders, conquering those who would illegally enter his country, and sending them off to captivity, thus preserving the traditional way of life in Egypt.

The carvings reveal clues to the physical characteristics of the Philistines during the time of the biblical judges—

Name: Medinet Habu wall relief
Origin and date: Thebes ~1156 BC
Present location: Theban Necropolis, Egypt

such as Samson, who was a contemporary (Judges 14:1). The reliefs also give an insight into the fashion, employment, clothing, weaponry, instruments, modes of transportation, and livestock of the Philistines and other Sea Peoples.

Even though the relief at Ramesses III's mortuary temple was intended to portray his defeat of the Sea Peoples rather than their migration into Egypt and Canaan at the time of the judges, it does show us that the Bible's record of the Philistines being on the eastern Mediterranean seaboard, which includes Canaan, at the beginning of Iron Age 1 (1200 to 1000 BC) is true.

Medinet Habu, the mortuary temple of Ramesses III

MONARCHY

15 HOUSE OF DAVID STELE

First Archaeological Mention of David

Up until 1993, not one shred of evidence existed outside the pages of the Bible for one of the most central figures of the Old Testament—King David. Though he's mentioned over 1,000 times in the Bible and is the listed author of 73 psalms, David hadn't shown up outside the Bible's record. The absence of archaeological evidence emboldened many to state that King David never existed and was a figment of the imagination of a post-exilic Jewish community. Presumably, after the Israelites returned to Jerusalem from Babylonian captivity in the fifth century BC, they invented David as a national figure the depleted nation could rally around as they rebuilt their country. For example, British scholar Philip R. Davies said, "The figure of King David is about as historical as King Arthur."[1]

All that changed when a chance discovery was made at the ruins of the ancient city of Dan in northern Israel. The site of Dan is identified with Tel Dan. It is situated at the foot of Mount Hermon on the fringes of the northeast corner of the Huleh Valley. It's a large site, over 50 acres in area, and is located at the important junction of the ancient crossroads of the Great Trunk Route and the Via Maris.

In 1993, Gila Cook, a member of a team led by archaeologist Avraham Biran, found three fragments of an Aramaic inscription on broken stones used to build a wall

Name: Tel Dan Stele
Origin and date: Dan 9th c. BC
Discovered: Gila Cook 1993
Size: width 8.7 inches, height 12.6 inches
Present location: Israel Museum

in Tel Dan. The fragments date to about 100 years after the death of King David. They're a portion of a monument erected by Hazael, king of Aram-Damascus, which he inscribed with his proclamation of victory over "the House of David." Hazael conquered Israel and turned the nation into a vassal state (2 Kings 10:32). The stele was likely written as a memorial to this accomplishment.

This is the first time the term House of David has for certain been discovered outside the pages of the Bible, although some scholars argue David is mentioned on the Mesha Stele. Once the Israelites regained control of Dan, they likely smashed Hazael's monument. Someone later placed some of the broken pieces of the stele into the walls of the gate, where they remained in their secondary use for over 2,800 years. Even though more of the stele is missing than has been found, a reconstruction of lines seven to nine read, "I killed Jehoram son of Ahab king of Israel and I killed Ahaz-iahu son of Jehoram king of the House of David."

This incredible artifact, now on display at the Israel Museum, testifies to the existence of the founder of the Davidic dynasty, again demonstrating the historical accuracy of the Bible.

63

16 ARK OF THE COVENANT

The Ark of the Covenant is one of the most famous lost historical artifacts. Although its discovery is yet to occur, intriguing clues point to where it might be.

It was common for temples in the ancient Near East to have a designated space for sacred religious objects that were considered the property of the deity worshiped there. According to the Bible, the temple in Jerusalem built by King Solomon had such designated storage areas hidden from the public eye in the bowels of the Temple Mount (1 Kings 7:51). It was in secret chambers like these, the whereabouts of which were guarded by a select few, that the Ark of the Covenant could have been hidden before the final Babylonian invasion of Judah in 586 BC. This in-cursion culminated in the destruction of Jerusalem and Solomon's Temple (2 Kings 25:8-9).

King Nebuchadnezzar, following the standard modus operandi of the time, brought whatever conquered temple treasures he could locate back to Babylon as trophies of war. Even though long lists of the temple treasures taken by Nebuchadnezzar are given in the Bible (e.g., 2 Kings 25:13-17), there's no mention in the Bible or in Babylonian sources of Nebuchadnezzar bringing back the Ark of the Covenant as spoil.

After 70 years, the pilfered items were returned to the Jews by King Cyrus of Persia to be utilized in the rebuilt Jewish temple (Ezra 1:7-11). Since Cyrus had an inventory of the temple treasures taken by Nebuchadnezzar, he made sure every one of the 5,400 objects was returned to the Jews. But again, no mention was made of the Ark of the Covenant.

Jewish sources in the Second Temple period tell us that after the Ark of the Covenant went missing, the Holy of Holies, the Ark's former resting place, remained empty. All that remained in the holy spot was a stone jutting above the ground at the height of three fingers. This is where the Ark of the Covenant once stood and where the Muslim Dome of the Rock is today.

Based on more than a millennium of Jewish tradition, Maimonides, the 12th-century AD Jewish sage, stated that when Solomon built the first Jewish temple, he was aware it would ultimately be destroyed. Therefore, he constructed a chamber in which the Ark of the Covenant could be hidden below the temple surface in deep maze-like vaults.

About 1,000 years before Maimonides, the Jewish Mishnah stated that Israelite King Josiah hid the Ark of the Covenant in the seventh century BC in a secret underground tunnel that began underneath an area on the Temple Mount called the wood storage area. This area is perhaps located halfway between the site of the former Holy of Holies (now Dome of the Rock) and the modern-day Golden Gate.

This underground vault is known as chamber five. The chamber, some 40 feet underground, was last explored in 1865 by the English archaeologist Charles Wilson. He wrote the following about his explorations: "A low doorway cut in the rock leads to a flight of steps… the passage is covered by a semicircular vault, and at its entrance to the cistern are the remains of a doorway…blocked up by earth."[2]

The most famous archaeological object that remains undiscovered could still be resting quietly in the subterranean chambers behind this dirt-sealed doorway just below the hustle and bustle of the pilgrims daily touring the Temple Mount.

Tunnel under the Western Wall, Jerusalem

17 Holy of Holies

On the moon-like surface underneath one of the most spectacular buildings in the world, the 1,300-year-old Dome of the Rock, are clues that pinpoint the exact location where the Holy of Holies once stood. This famous site, where Solomon's Temple and then Herod's Temple were built, was last surveyed over 100 years ago by German scholar Gustaf Dalman, who was allowed in 1910 to inspect and measure the spot where the Ark of the Covenant was placed in the Jewish temple.

Through Dalman's observations and modern-day pictures taken by tourists inside the Dome of the Rock, a keen eye can detect numerous interesting features. For example, Temple Mount expert Leen Ritmeyer has pointed out the scarps (remains) from the walls of the Holy of Holies, which are exactly 20 cubits apart, the prescribed measurement given in the Bible (2 Chronicles 3:8). One can recognize the modifications made to the rock over the millennia. For example, there's evidence of Crusader quarrying. Pieces of the actual floor of the Holy of Holies were sold for their weight in gold as relics to help fund the Crusaders' campaigns.

Temple Mount, Jerusalem

View of the rock from above

The most astonishing circumstance is that despite the numerous modifications, we can see the rectangular basin or depression measuring four feet four inches by two feet seven inches (or 2.5 by 1.5 cubits) where the Ark of the Covenant stood for 400 years in Solomon's Temple (971-586 BC, according to conservative dating). This depression is located in the center of the Dome of the Rock, which was built over the Holy of Holies, and has the exact dimensions of the Ark given in the Bible (Exodus 25:10).

Because the Israelites would never have risked the Ark wobbling and falling over on the uneven bedrock surface, they built a basin for it to rest in. According to Ritmeyer, this fits with the biblical explanation King Solomon gave: "[I] have built an house for the name of the LORD God of Israel. And I have set there a place for the ark" (1 Kings 8:20-21). There's an incontrovertible connection between the rock and Israelite history. The Temple Mount Sifting Project (see page 106) and the biblical record provide an overwhelming indication of the existence of a Jewish temple on this holy place.

Solomon's Temple and the Ark of the Covenant were once here. There's proof of this even in the 21st century.

Inside the Dome of the Rock, Jerusalem

69

18 SOLOMON'S GATES

By far, the largest Old Testament period of Israelite construction took place during Solomon's reign, thereby indicating his control and protection over the coveted International Highway that traced the Fertile Crescent. According to the Bible, Solomon ordered his vassals to labor projects that included building the temple and his palace in Jerusalem (1 Kings 6–7), as well as construction at hub cities located at crucial points on the north-south axis of the International Highway in northern Israel.

Archaeological evidence discovered in three major cities of ancient Israel—Hazor, Megiddo, and Gezer—validate the biblical account of Solomon rebuilding these

Hazor royal fortress gate

Six-chambered gate at Tel Gezer

Gates at Tel Megiddo

cities, which were spaced throughout Israel at key junctures (1 Kings 9:15). They were strategic administrative centers that controlled the major road junctions. These building projects helped transition the nation of Israel from a country of primarily shepherds and farmers to a regional superpower with international trade connections.

Archaeologists discovered similar building features at these three cities' gates that conclusively date their construction to the 10th century BC. This is of tremendous importance for demonstrating the historical accuracy of the biblical account of Solomon's building projects. Archaeologists discovered that each of these three cities built during the Solomonic period had a casemate wall, which was a new technology that used a double wall to protect a city. Each had a large gate with six chambers, three on either side, with two huge towers guarding the city's entryway. The pottery discovered in the gates' strata attests to these fortifications being built at the time of King Solomon.

The casemate wall, the specifics of the gate plan used in just one period of Israelite history—Solomon's building—and the dating of the pottery confirm that each of these cities was constructed by Solomon at the same time as the Bible records. Again, the archaeological data confirm in detail the historicity of the biblical account.

Cutting Down Cedars for the Construction of the Temple, Gustave Dore

19 MESHA STELE

Numerous archaeological discoveries relate to the Israelite King Omri, who reigned for 12 years over the northern kingdom of Israel (approximately 884–873 BC). Though the Bible gives Omri little attention compared to other kings, the artifacts shed light on his reign.

In the first-ever mention of an Israelite king found outside the pages of the Bible, the name Omri appears on the Mesha Stele, also known as the Moabite Stone. Some scholars argue that King David is also mentioned, although damage to that portion of the stele has made the determination difficult. The stele dates to the time of Ahab, the son and successor of Omri, around 846 BC. Frederick Augustus Klein, an Anglican missionary, discovered the stele in 1868 in what is now modern-day Dhiban, Jordan. Hearing about it, archaeologist Charles Clermont-Ganneau, based at the French consulate in Jerusalem, sent people to gather more information.

The stele was shattered by local Arabs in 1869, who baked it in a fire and then threw cold water on it to prevent the stone being taken from them. Fortunately, one of Clermont-Ganneau's intermediaries had made a papier-mâché impression prior to its destruction. Clermont-Ganneau located many of the fragments and reconstructed much of the original stele, which is now on display in the Louvre.

Name: Mesha Stele or Moabite Stone
Origin and date: Dibon ~846 BC
Discovered: Frederick Augustus Klein 1868
Size: width 2 feet, height ~3 feet
Present location: Louvre, France

The Mesha Stele, which also mentions the name of the Hebrew God YHWH, describes from the perspective of Mesha, king of Moab, how, with the favor of the god Chemosh, Moab was delivered from Israelite subjugation: "Omri had occupied the land of Medeba." According to the Bible, Omri and his son Ahab subjected Mesha to a tax of 100,000 lambs and the wool of 100,000 rams annually (2 Kings 3:4). The port city of Tyre offered Israel a commercial outlet for the wool. Tyre needed textiles in order to produce their famous purple-dyed products. The purpose of the stele is indicated in lines three and four, where King Mesha says that he erected the stele at the high place of Qarhoh (the main citadel) to venerate Chemosh.

Approximately five years later, Omri's name was recorded on another object, the famous Black Obelisk of Shalmaneser III (840 BC). Assyrian King Shalmaneser III (approximately 859–824 BC) not only refers to the next king of Israel, Jehu, as the "son of Omri," but the obelisk also provides Jehu's picture, the only image of an Israelite king ever discovered. Even 100 years after Omri's death, his reign was remembered by a series of famous Assyrian kings like Tiglath-Pileser III and Sargon II, who mentioned the northern kingdom of Israel as Omri-Land.

These discoveries related to Omri help confirm the historical reliability of the biblical record.

20 JEZEBEL'S SEAL

A Child's Story of the Bible—2.
JEZEBEL, WIFE OF KING AHAB

A small but spectacular archaeological discovery relates to one of the Bible's most infamous villains. That item is the personal seal of the Israelite queen Jezebel, which she would have pressed into clay as her signature.

In the 9th century BC, the friendly relations between Omri, king of northern Israel, and Ethobaal, king of Tyre, culminated in the marriage of their children Ahab and Jezebel (1 Kings 16:31). With the marriage, Israel made a political and economic alliance with Phoenicia.

This was the perfect time for Israel to have access to the Phoenician port city of Tyre because it was the main seaport and maritime powerhouse in the ancient Near East. Importing and exporting just about everything under the sun, Tyre offered Israel a commercial outlet for agricultural products from the Valley of Jezreel. From here they could supply food to the large populace in Tyre and the eastern Mediterranean seaboard. And it also gave Ahab a purchaser for the 100,000 lambs and the wool of 100,000 rams he received in tribute from Mesha, king of Moab (2 Kings 3:4).

But the royal couple, especially Jezebel, were notorious for their persecution of Israelites who were faithful to YHWH and refused to bend the knee to the Canaanite storm god Baal, whom

Jezebel (meaning "where is his highness Baal") was named after. According to the Bible, while Jezebel was slaughtering YHWH's prophets, a devout believer of YHWH named Obadiah was hiding many prophets in caves and supplying them with food and water (1 Kings 18:4).

The most famous of her rivals was the prophet of YHWH Elijah, whom Jezebel hunted in every surrounding kingdom and nation. In poetic justice, the bloodthirsty Jezebel died a horrific death by being thrown from a window at her winter capital of Jezreel. Her blood was spattered on the wall, and horses trampled her underfoot. Then to add insult to injury, and to fulfill a prophecy made by Elijah, wild dogs devoured Jezebel's flesh, leaving only her skull, her feet, and her hands to be buried (1 Kings 21:23; 2 Kings 9:30-37).

It's not known where in the Holy Land the seal was found because it was given to Israel's Department of Antiquities by an anonymous donor in the 1960s. The slightly broken seal, which is large for a personal seal, measures 1.25 inches high. Not only does the seal have the name Jezebel, or (L')YZBL, inscribed upon it, it also contains many rare and interesting features fit only for a queen.

Name: opal seal with the name Jezebel
Origin and date: unknown
Discovered: early 1960s
Size: height 1.24 inches
Present location: Israel Museum

At the top of the seal is a crouching winged Egyptian sphinx with the face of a woman. To the left of the sphinx is an ankh, the Egyptian symbol of life. Below this is a line that has a winged disk and an Egyptian falcon flanked by cobras, a common symbol of the Egyptian/Phoenician monarchy. Below the falcon is a lotus, a common symbol of a female. Then the name YZBL is inscribed at the four points surrounding the falcon. At the top of the broken seal were probably the two Hebrew letters *lamed*, short for "(belonging) to," and *aleph*, the first but missing letter in Jezebel's name.

Jezebel is the Phoenician queen of ancient Israel, from Guillaume Rouillé's Promptuarii Iconum Insigniorum, *1553*

The discovery of the personal seal of one of the greatest villains in the Bible once again strengthens confidence in the historical accuracy of the biblical record.

77

21 BLACK OBELISK

Picture of an Israelite King

Found deep under the sands of the ancient Assyrian city of Calah (Nimrud), the Black Obelisk of Shalmaneser III contains the only known picture of an ancient Israelite king. This object almost wasn't found. In 1846, dig leader Austen Henry Layard resisted the petitions of his workers to stop excavating the site and instead continued digging for one more day. That day they found the Black Obelisk, which is now on display at the British Museum.

The impressive four-sided obelisk is polished black limestone measuring six feet six inches high, with five panels of small pictures on each side. There are 190 lines of ancient cuneiform text on the obelisk that describe the triumphs of Assyrian King Shalmaneser III (approximately 857–826 BC). This king is also mentioned in the Bible (2 Kings 17:3). The snapshot panels depict the king receiving exotic tribute—camels, an elephant, monkeys, apes, and perhaps a rhinoceros, all of which could have been put in a royal zoo.

One of the panels depicts a man prostrating himself, a symbolic representation of the complete subjugation of himself and his kingdom. Behind him is a group of servants offering tribute to Shalmaneser III. The text written above this panel identifies this defeated dignitary as none other than the king of the northern kingdom of Israel,

Name: Black Obelisk of Shalmaneser III
Origin and date: Nimrud 827–824 BC
Discovered: Austen Henry Layard 1846
Size: width ~18 inches, height 6.5 feet
Present location: British Museum

"Jehu, the son of Omri." Thanks to the ancient Assyrian stone carvers and the chance find of this object, we have the only known image of an Israelite king.

Jehu was not of royal lineage but was a commander of the Israelite army. After being anointed king by the prophet Elisha, Jehu waged a coordinated attack and killed Joram, king of Israel, and Ahaziah, king of Judah. Jezebel, the queen of Israel, and all of Ahab's family were also executed (2 Kings 9–10). Thus, Jehu effectively eradicated Baal worship from Israel. He then seized the throne of the northern kingdom of Israel in the capital city of Samaria, and, likely in order to make his throne more secure, he submitted himself to the superpower of the time, the Assyrian kingdom, and its leader, Shalmaneser. This submission is so wonderfully illustrated on the Black Obelisk.

This extrabiblical discovery mentioning and portraying Jehu demonstrates that the historical accuracy of the Bible stands up to scrutiny.

22 ISAIAH'S SEAL

Archaeological evidence has been found proving the existence of the writer of one of the most famous Messianic passages in the Old Testament. Isaiah 53 is quoted in the first six books of the New Testament and by 1 Peter as a prophecy that was fulfilled by Jesus, the Jewish Messiah.

In 2018, excavations in the Ophel, the raised area between the City of David and the Temple Mount, produced a fragmented clay bulla, or round seal, dating to the eighth or seventh century BC and inscribed with the name of the prophet Isaiah. In the ancient Near East, seals were often engraved with the owner's name and could function as a legal signature. Seals were used by most classes of society and were usually pressed into wet clay instead of soft wax because clay hardens and maintains

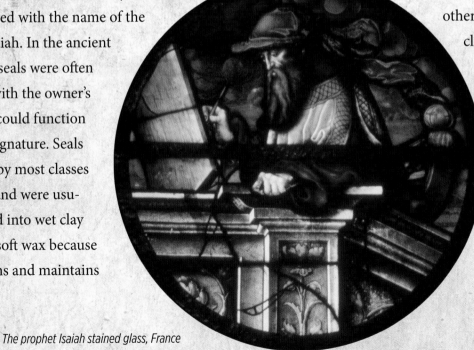

The prophet Isaiah stained glass, France

its shape when heated, while wax melts.

Just south of the most controversial 35 acres of real estate in the world, the Temple Mount, archaeologists found Isaiah's seal a short distance from where they had found a seal in 2015 bearing the name of Hezekiah, the king of Judah, a contemporary of Isaiah. The seal of Isaiah was discovered by wet sifting, a form of analysis to separate coarse or abrasive material with high-pressured water to discover small artifacts that would have otherwise been encased within a clump of earth and missed.

On the top of Isaiah's seal is what appears to be a doe or some other four-legged animal. Underneath are two incomplete Hebrew words. Though two of the eight Hebrew letters in the first word are missing, it most certainly spells out "belonging to Isaiah." The line below it undoubtedly spells out "prophet," even though one of the four letters is missing. No other sequence of letters makes any grammatical or historical sense; this is the personal seal of the prophet Isaiah.

Through the wealth of data unearthed by archaeologists in Jerusalem, we are able to measure the Bible's historical accuracy. Isaiah the prophet really did live in the eighth to seventh centuries BC, and his prophecies concerning Christ's virgin birth (Isaiah 7:14), sufferings, and exaltation (Isaiah 52:13–53:12) came to pass in the first century AD, as will Isaiah's prophecies concerning the end of the world, the second coming of Christ, and the establishment of the Messiah's kingdom in Jerusalem.

Name: Isaiah's seal
Origin and date: Ophel ~700 BC
Discovered: Eilat Mazar 2018
Size: width .5 inch

*Isaiah's Vision of the Destruction of Babylon
(Isaiah 13:19-22), Gustave Dore*

23 UZZIAH BURIAL MARKER

Archaeological evidence has been discovered that confirms the existence of Uzziah, the eighth-century king of Jerusalem. Uzziah, sometimes called Azariah (2 Kings 15:6), oversaw a renaissance of sorts in the southern kingdom of Judah. The ancient Near Eastern superpowers of the day, such as Assyria and Egypt, were waning in their influence, and Uzziah took the opportunity to expand Judah's power beyond its own borders into neighboring countries like Philistia, Edom, and Arabia.

The kingdom of Judah also took the geopolitical opportunity to refortify its critical infrastructure. For example, Uzziah rebuilt the important port city of Ezion-Geber, near modern-day Eilat on the Red Sea (2 Kings 14:22). It was a time of greatness for the south and its capital city of Jerusalem.

Tragically, in a moment of pride, Uzziah lost it all by overstepping the divine boundaries that separated the functions of the monarchy from that of the priesthood. King Uzziah decided to take on the role of the high priest by offering incense to YHWH in the temple in Jerusalem (2 Chronicles 26:16). According to the Bible, the combined office of king/priest is reserved for the Messiah alone (Psalm 110:4; Hebrews 6:20). Consequently, Uzziah was punished with leprosy and forced to live out the rest of his days in humiliation and isolation (2 Kings 15:5).

Because he was smitten by YHWH with leprosy, the king was considered unclean and cursed even upon his

King Uzziah Stricken with Leprosy, Rembrandt

82

Name: Uzziah burial marker
Origin and date: Jerusalem ~AD 50
Discovered: E. L. Sukenik 1931
Size: width ~13.4 inches, height ~13.8 inches
Present location: Israel Museum

death. Therefore, he wasn't permitted to be buried with the other kings of Jerusalem in the royal cemetery but rather had a special plot close to the royal tombs (2 Chronicles 26:23).

In 1931, Israeli archaeologist E. L. Sukenik, best known for helping establish the Department of Antiquities at Hebrew University, discovered a burial marker for Uzziah by chance. It was found among a collection of other artifacts at a Russian Orthodox convent in Jerusalem. The burial marker was created around the time of Jesus, about 700 years after Uzziah's death. The marker indicates that the bones of the cursed king were moved from their original location to another tomb for an unspecified reason. The marker, which at one time sealed the tomb, is engraved in ancient Hebrew and reads "Here were brought the bones of Uzziah, king of Judah. Do not open!"

Uzziah's burial marker is on display at the Israel Museum in Jerusalem.

24 HEZEKIAH'S SEAL

A small but stunning archaeological find is linked to one of the most well-known kings of Jerusalem, Hezekiah. In 2015, excavations in the Ophel, the raised area between the City of David and the Temple Mount, produced a clay bulla, or round seal, dating to the eighth century BC inscribed with the name of Hezekiah. Other seals bearing his name have been known to archaeologists from the black market, which can bring their authenticity into question, but this was the first-ever discovery of any Israelite king's seal found during a proper archaeological excavation.

In the world of the Bible, seals were often engraved with the name of the owner, along with other decorations. They were required to authenticate important transactions and were necessary for royalty like Hezekiah to validate royal decrees (compare Daniel 6:17). Seals were frequently worn on a chain around the neck or inserted into armlets or finger rings (Song of Solomon 8:6).

The Hezekiah seal was at one time inserted into a ring, as the depressions around the seal demonstrate. The tiny seal, about half an inch in diameter, was one of over 30 seals found in the same location, a refuse dump next to the remains of what was at one time likely a Judean royal administrative center near the Temple Mount.

Name: Hezekiah's seal
Origin and date: Ophel 8th c. BC
Discovered: Eilat Mazar 2015
Size: diameter .5 inch

King Hezekiah from Guillaume Rouillé's Promptuarii Iconum Insigniorum, *1553*

King Hezekiah, clothed in sackcloth, spreads open the letter threatening Assyrian invasion before the Lord (2 Kings 19:14). From The Story of the Bible from Genesis to Revelation

Like the seal of Isaiah the prophet, a contemporary of Hezekiah, Hezekiah's seal was discovered by wet sifting, a technique using high-pressured water to separate coarse or abrasive material to find small artifacts. The seal reads in ancient Hebrew "Belonging to Hezekiah (son of) Ahaz king of Judah." It's decorated with familiar royal motifs: a two-winged Egyptian sun with the wings pointed downward, and ankhs, a symbol of life, flanking either side.

Through the wealth of data unearthed by archaeologists in Jerusalem, such as Hezekiah's seal, we're able to measure the Bible's historical accuracy. Hezekiah really did live in the eighth century BC and really was a contemporary of Isaiah, who together with him strove to persuade the nation of Israel, who walked in darkness, to see the light of YHWH.

King Hezekiah on his sickbed (2 Kings 20:1)

25　Hezekiah's Tunnel

Pilgrims to the Holy Land can visit and even walk through an incredible feat of engineering—a tunnel cut through solid rock that dates to approximately 700 BC and brings to life a famous biblical account.

On the verge of Jerusalem being attacked by King Sennacherib and the Assyrian army, King Hezekiah undertook a major building project to ensure that Jerusalem's water supply would continue to flow in the case of a siege. He had a tunnel hewn out of bedrock, essentially a closed aqueduct, that wound its way through the belly of the City of David. Water from the Gihon Spring, which was located outside the city walls and thus vulnerable to an invading enemy, was redirected through the 1,750-foot conduit to the Pool of Siloam safely within the ancient city walls of Jerusalem.

The American biblical scholar Edward Robinson was the first person to explore the tunnel in modern times (1838), but it was a local boy named Jacob Spafford, the adopted son of the hymnist Horatio Spafford, who, while playing in the tunnel in 1880, stumbled upon an important ancient Hebrew inscription. The inscription is significant not only because it validates the biblical account but also

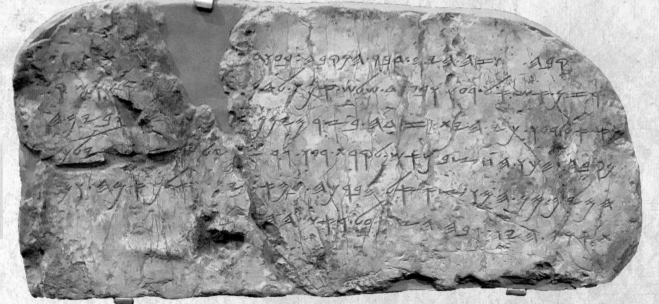

Name: Siloam Inscription
Origin and date: Jerusalem ~700 BC
Discovered: Jacob Spafford 1880
Size: width 4.3 feet, height 8.3 inches
Present location: Istanbul
Archaeological Museum

because it's the only inscription from ancient Israel that commemorates a public works program. It is also one of the oldest examples of Hebrew writing.

The boy brought his discovery to the attention of the authorities, who unprofessionally removed the inscription, resulting in irreparable damage. The Siloam Inscription is the laborers' description of their cutting of the tunnel. Two groups worked toward each other from opposite ends, the source and the reservoir. They connected the separate ends of the tunnel, and at the spot where they met, they inscribed a plaque commemorating their tremendous feat.

This accomplishment is mentioned numerous times in the Bible in connection with Hezekiah's fortification preparations against Sennacherib's attack (2 Kings 20:20). The Siloam Inscription is stored at the Istanbul Archaeology Museum in Turkey because it was discovered when Israel was under the dominion of the Ottoman Empire (AD 1517–1917).

Hezekiah's tunnel, which still brings water into Jerusalem, was an incredible engineering accomplishment. Along with the epigraphical evidence of the Siloam Inscription, the tunnel demonstrates the historical reliability of the biblical account.

26 HEZEKIAH'S BROAD WALL

A massive archaeological discovery related to Hezekiah sheds light on how the king prepared Jerusalem for the coming war with the superpower of the day, Assyria.

When Hezekiah began his reign as king of Judah around 715 BC, the neighboring northern kingdom of Israel had been crushed by Assyria (approximately 721 BC), and the Jewish population there had been deported (2 Kings 17:22-23). Knowing that the kingdom of Judah was next in Assyria's path as its army made its way along the Fertile Crescent to Egypt, Hezekiah quickly began major building projects to protect Jerusalem from the imminent Assyrian invasion.

According to the Bible, Hezekiah constructed a tunnel beneath Jerusalem to bring water from the Gihon Spring outside the city walls to the Pool of Siloam inside the walls. He also built a new wall around Jerusalem to protect his subjects who lived in nearby unwalled villages and who would need to come to the city for safety. This wall would also provide another line of defense in the upcoming war (2 Chronicles 32:5).

Name: Hezekiah's Broad Wall
Origin and date: Jerusalem ~700 BC
Discovered: Nahman Avigad 1970s
Size: length 140 feet, width 23 feet, height 10.8 feet
Present location: Jerusalem's Old City

A portion of this wall was found by Israeli archaeologist Nahman Avigad in the 1970s during excavations of the Old City of Jerusalem conducted from 1969 to 1982. It has proven to be the most massive and important Iron Age 2 (1000–586 BC) architectural remains ever discovered in Jerusalem. The remnants of the wall consist mostly of its foundations. The pottery found in situ help date its construction to the time of Hezekiah. Of special note is the discovery of residential houses Hezekiah expropriated and demolished in a sort of equivalent to modern-day eminent domain so the engineers would have enough material to reinforce the new wall.

This discovery lines up exactly with Isaiah the prophet's proclamation against Jerusalem (Isaiah 22:10). Like many other ancient walls, this one is composed of large unhewn fieldstones. But unlike other walls found in Israel, it's massive, hence the name the Broad Wall. The 140-foot-long portion that's been unearthed measures 23 feet across, and the foundations were preserved in part to over 10 feet high.

The discovery of the Broad Wall in Jerusalem, which can be viewed by tourists, demonstrates again the historical reliability of the biblical account.

27 THE SILVER SCROLLS
Oldest Bible Verses in the World

In 1979, a team of Israeli archaeologists led by Dr. Gabriel Barkay was surveying rock-hewn burial chambers in Ketef Hinnom. This is an archaeological site in the Hinnom Valley just outside the walls of Jerusalem on the ancient route from Jerusalem to Bethlehem. What they found is one of the most significant biblical discoveries ever made—the oldest Bible text uncovered so far.

After surveying what's known as cave 24, the archaeologists decided the cave was empty and moved on to survey another nearby cave. A local 13-year-old boy who had been tagging along with the team of archaeologists stayed back and did what most teenage boys might do. He found a tool and started digging in the ground. At the time, the archaeologists hadn't realized that an earthquake had occurred some 2,600 years before, causing the cave's ceiling to collapse and the contents of the cave to stay in situ on the floor, frozen in time for over two millennia.

The boy dug a small hole and hit pay dirt. He brought some of the unearthed objects to the archaeologists, who soon conducted an excavation. Among the most spectacular finds were two silver objects measuring 1.1 by 3.8 inches and .4 by 1.5 inches that are now known as KH1 and KH2, respectively.

It took the archaeologists three years to unroll them because of their extremely fragile state. The long process was worth the wait since the silver scrolls, which were probably amulets or charms worn on a necklace, were found to be engraved

with Numbers 6:24-26. This is the earliest known inscription from the Hebrew Bible.

The passage is called the Priestly Blessing. It begins by beseeching God to bestow physical and spiritual blessings upon His people and to keep or protect them from all evil. The prayer continues by petitioning God to make His face or nature favorable toward the children of Israel and to be kind to them. Finally, the benediction asks God to be a source of comfort to His people and to bless them with peace.

By using the pottery found near the silver scrolls to help date them, archaeologists determined that they're from the sixth century BC, making them some 400 years older than the previously known oldest Bible texts in the world, the Dead Sea Scrolls. The opening of the brittle scrolls clearly revealed a word-for-word copy of the famous Numbers 6:24-26 blessing, along with portions of other familiar verses in the Torah.

This is another instance where the findings of archaeology confirm the historical accuracy of the Bible. This discovery is now on display in the Israel Museum in Jerusalem.

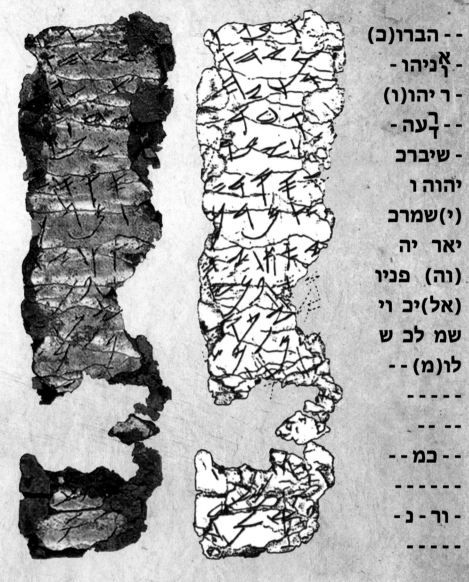

- - הברו(כ)
-אָ‎ניהו -
- ר יהו(ו)
- - כָ‎עה -
- שיברכ
יהוה ו
(י)שמרכ
יאר יה
(וה) פניו
(אל)יכ וי
שמ לכ ש
לו(מ) - -
- - - - -
- - - -
- - כמ - -
- - - - -
ור - נ -
- - - - -

Name: Ketef Hinnom scrolls
Origin and date: Jerusalem 6th c. BC
Discovered: Gabriel Barkay 1979
Size: 1.1 x 3.8 inches and .4 x 1.5 inches
Present location: Israel Museum

28 TAHARQA SPHINX

Archaeological evidence has come to light demonstrating the historicity of one of the pharaohs mentioned in the Bible. The Black Pharaohs were a line of rulers from the 25th dynasty of Egypt who originated in ancient Nubia, or modern-day northern Sudan, and ruled over Egypt for about 100 years. Taharqa, also spelled Tirhakah, was one of them.

According to the biblical account, after King Sennacherib of Assyria overthrew the Israelite town of Lachish, he went on to attack the nearby city of Libnah. A field commander told him they'd intercepted intelligence that King Hezekiah of Judah had made a pact with Tirhakah to make war with Assyria from the south (2 Kings 19:8-9). The Black Pharaohs were initially neutral in the war between Assyria and Judah, but foreseeing the inevitable result, they came to Judah's aid. In the end, God Himself saved Judah, and Sennacherib retreated to Nineveh (2 Kings 19:35-36).

The most prominent object found that relates to this pharaoh is the Sphinx of Taharqa. The granite statue, which has Egyptian and Kushite elements in its design, was found

Name: Sphinx of Taharqa
Origin and date: Nubia ~680 BC
Discovered: Francis Llewellyn Griffith 1932
Size: length 28.7 inches, height 16 inches
Present location: British Museum

at the Temple of Amun in ancient Nubia, now Sudan. It's a highlighted object on display at the British Museum.

The existence of Tirhakah is also testified to by later historians. The Black Pharaoh is mentioned by Manetho, the third-century BC Egyptian priest/historian who authored the book *The History of Egypt*, which was the gold standard for chronicling the reigns of Egyptian pharaohs. Tirhakah is also mentioned by the first-century BC Greek historian Strabo.

The discovery of archaeological objects related to Taharqa is significant because all three of the kings mentioned in 2 Kings 19—Sennacherib, Hezekiah, and Taharqa—have been proven to exist from extrabiblical archaeological sources. This affirms yet again the historical accuracy of the biblical account.

Ram sphinx of Taharqa in the British Museum

Head of Pharaoh Taharqa in the Nubian Museum

29 POLYDACTYLISM
Physical Anomalies in the World of the Bible

Gilgamesh

Archaeological evidence has surfaced that not only demonstrates the ancients' knowledge of physical anomalies like polydactylism—a condition in humans and animals resulting in extra fingers and/or toes—but also sheds light on the reliability of the biblical record.

2 Samuel 21:20 mentions a Philistine warrior from Gath with six fingers on each hand and six toes on each foot. He also had "great stature" and was descended from a giant. The Israelites apparently believed that polydactylism was a characteristic of giants or people with almost superhuman strength. Scripture references many people who would be considered abnormally tall or strong today. One such person was Nimrod, who established Babel after the Flood and was described as "a mighty one in the earth" (Genesis 10:8). His exploits are reflected in legends such as Gilgamesh, an ancient Mesopotamian hero who's been associated with Nimrod.

There's ample archaeological evidence demonstrating polydactylism in numerous ancient Near Eastern cultures. An example from the Holy Land comes from the city of Jericho, where archaeologists discovered a statue of a person with six toes. Another example is an anthropoid sarcophagus found at the ancient Egyptian outpost city of Deir-el-Balah that depicts the encased deceased with six fingers on each hand.

At the other end of the Fertile Crescent, archaeologists discovered a seventh-century BC text called *Summa Izbu* (anomalous birth) in the library of Ashurbanipal, the Assyrian king mentioned in Ezra 4:10. This Assyrian text interprets polydactylism to be either good luck or bad luck depending on whether the extra fingers or toes were on the left hand or foot or the right hand or foot.

In modern society, polydactylism is rarely observed in people outside the Third World because extra fingers or toes are usually medically removed early in life. But in antiquity, as demonstrated by the Bible and archaeological representations from cultures at both ends of the Fertile Crescent, the anomaly existed and was recognized. Six-fingered giants reaching nine feet tall as mentioned in the Bible may sound implausible to many in our modern society, but ancient manuscripts and archaeological objects have demonstrated that unique people existed.

Christian, the polydactyl cat belonging to the author's daughter, Hosanna Meyer

Woodcut illustration from the Nuremberg Chronicle showing a man with 12 fingers

95

30 HOUSE OF BULLAE

Seals of People Mentioned in Jeremiah

Archaeological evidence from the City of David in Jerusalem confirms the existence of some of the most obscure people mentioned in the Bible, thus proving again that the Bible's historical accuracy stands up to scrutiny.

In 1982, Israeli archaeologists were excavating the layer of ruins from the time of Jerusalem's destruction by Babylon in 586 BC. In a place that's now been labeled the House of Bullae, they discovered over 50 bullae or seals dating to the time of Jeremiah the prophet. The room at one time stored numerous papyrus documents, but these ancient texts were destroyed by conflagration and only the clay seals remained.

The Prophet Jeremiah in the Sistine Chapel, Michelangelo

A bulla is a lump of clay that has a seal impression of the owner on it. Bullae were used for the purpose of sealing or authenticating important documents. One of these bullae lists a person named "Gemariah the son of Shaphan." This same person is mentioned almost in passing in the Bible as an official scribe under the administration of King Jehoiakim (Jeremiah 36:10-12). He's probably best known for pleading with that wicked king

Name: House of Bullae seals
Origin and date: Jerusalem 7th to 6th c. BC
Discovered: Yigal Shiloh 1982
Size: varied
Present location: Israel Museum

not to burn the scroll of Jeremiah that contained prophecies concerning the disasters YHWH was about to inflict upon the kingdom of Judah (Jeremiah 36:25).

Two different seals carry the name "Baruch son of Neriah," who was Jeremiah's friend and scribe (Jeremiah 36:4). One of the seals has even proven to have a fingerprint on it. It's possibly the fingerprint of Baruch himself, the person to whom Jeremiah dictated his ominous prophecies concerning the doom coming to Judah.

The discovery of objects bearing the names of Gemariah and Baruch are just two examples from over 100 cases in which archaeologists have found the name of a person recorded in the Bible that was written upon an object buried long ago. The discoveries of these artifacts mentioning lesser-known biblical characters demonstrate that these people really did exist, and the events surrounding their lives, in this instance the destruction of Jerusalem by fire in 586 BC, really did occur.

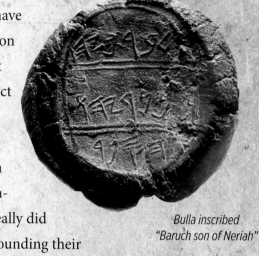

Bulla inscribed "Baruch son of Neriah"

House of Bullae, City of David, Jerusalem

97

31 SIEGE OF LACHISH RELIEFS

Of the many archaeological discoveries of objects bearing the names of people and places mentioned in the Bible, one of the most fantastic finds was by British archaeologist Austen Henry Layard. During excavations of ancient Nineveh between 1845 and 1847, Layard found a series of wall reliefs within the palace of King Sennacherib. These snapshot images portray one of Sennacherib's greatest military conquests. The 39-foot-long by 16.7-foot-high carving called the Siege of Lachish Relief is now on display at the British Museum. It portrays the Assyrian king's attack on the biblical city of Lachish.

This extrabiblical source shows in detailed imagery the same account mentioned in 2 Chronicles 32:9. It not only validates the biblical narrative but also fleshes out the biblical account. The relief depicts the Lachish fortress, the siege weapons, the Assyrian troops, the Jewish captives be-

Austen Henry Layard

Siege ramp, Lachish archaeological site

The Capture of Lachish

ing led away after the fall of the city, and Sennacherib himself at the head of his army.

Though the city of Lachish is scarcely mentioned in the Old Testament, it was second in importance only to Jerusalem for the southern kingdom of Judah because of its strategic location. As such, it was highly fortified. A huge retaining wall encircled Lachish to maintain the city's steep slopes and prevent erosion. A glacis, an artificial bank sloping away from the city, was built to expose enemies to Israelite archers on the walls. The gate was massive, the largest ever found from the period of the Israelite monarchy.

But despite Israel's best

Ancient Nineveh in modern-day northern Iraq

fortification efforts, Lachish was destroyed by the mighty Sennacherib in approximately 701 BC. In order to overthrow the seemingly impenetrable Israelite stronghold, Sennacherib's army constructed a siege ramp 200 feet wide and 250 feet long. Not only is this siege ramp portrayed in the Lachish reliefs, but the ramp is still in existence and is the only known Assyrian siege ramp left in the world.

The ramp was probably built by captured Israelites from conquered neighboring cities. The captives were forced to gather nearly 20,000 tons of fieldstones from the surrounding fields and build the ramp. Once in

place, the ramp's face was coated with a layer of stones bound by mortar. Siege machines were then positioned on the ramp, as can be seen in the relief, and the city was overthrown. Israelite archaeologists discovered the remains of weapons, ammunition, and equipment from this battle at the foot of the city wall.

The Lachish reliefs are one of the rare instances in which archaeologists have found an ancient "picture" to supplement an event described in the Bible.

Name: Lachish reliefs
Origin and date: Nineveh 700–681 BC
Discovered: Austen Henry Layard 1845–1847
Size: width 39 feet long, height up to 16.7 feet
Present location: British Museum

32 EKRON INSCRIPTION

A one-of-a-kind archaeological discovery has confirmed an Old Testament prophecy. Zephaniah was a court prophet who ministered in Jerusalem during the time of King Josiah (approximately 640–609 BC). He predicted the catastrophic results of the coming Babylonian invasion of Judah and the surrounding nations. The archrivals of Judah, the Philistines, were among the nations singled out for destruction (Zephaniah 2:4-5). Zephaniah said the Philistine city of Ekron would be rooted up in the invasion.

Israeli archaeologist Trude Dothan spent 14 seasons excavating what she thought to be Ekron, but she couldn't prove it. Then in 1996, archaeologists stumbled upon something unexpected. For the first time in archaeological history, they discovered a monumental inscription naming a biblical city and its kings in situ in a destruction layer that can be dated.

Dating to the seventh century BC, the Ekron inscription is complete and contains five lines of 71 letters that show a Phoenician influence. The short inscription commemorates the dedication of a Philistine sanctuary in a temple complex. It gives a list of five kings of Ekron along with a dedication to the temple's goddess. The destruction layer in which the archaeologists found the Ekron inscription is from 87 years later. It dates to around 603 BC, which is when the city was destroyed by Nebuchadnezzar of Babylon as Zephaniah had predicted.

Though it took years to correctly identify the Philistine city of Ekron and prove the city was indeed destroyed by the Babylonians as prophesied, the discovery validates the Bible's accuracy. In every case where the historicity of the biblical account can be tested, the Bible has demonstrated again and again that it is historically reliable.

Name: Ekron inscription
Origin and date: Ekron 7th c. BC
Discovered: Seymour Gitin and Trude Dothan 1996
Size: width 24 inches, height 15 inches
Present location: Israel Museum

EXILE

33   TEMPLE MOUNT SIFTING PROJECT

Jewish Historical Presence Confirmed

The Jewish Temple Mount, or Arabic Haram al-Sharif, is the centerpiece of the political conflict over Jerusalem. Any perceived provocation by the Jews is regarded as a blatant challenge to Arabs, the Muslim world, and the international community.

Starting in 1996 and going through the early 2000s, the Islamic Waqf, the Moslem Trust, and the Islamic Movement conducted a major construction operation on the southeast corner of the Temple Mount. This operation included a dig that inflicted much irreparable archaeological damage to the mount. These actions were part of a general trend by the Islamic Waqf to prevent any archaeological research that might reveal elements of the Jewish past there. Ikrima Sa'id Sabri, the Palestinian mufti (expert in religious law) of Jerusalem from

1994 to 2006, has stated:

> No stone of the Western Wall has any connection to Hebrew history....There is not the smallest indication of the existence of a Jewish temple on this place in the past. In the whole city, there is not even a single stone indicating Jewish history.... The Temple Mount was never there....There is not one bit of proof to establish that.[3]

The main goal of this construction project was to turn every vacant point on the mount into a mosque. The Waqf converted the underground chamber known as Solomon's Stables and the entrance to it into a mosque for prayer.

The excavated earth from this operation, bursting with archaeological data, was removed by heavy machinery and unceremoniously dumped by the truckload into the near-

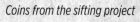

Coins from the sifting project

by Kidron Valley. Although the ancient finds there are not in situ, the soil still contains great historical potential. It's also the only archaeological information that's ever been available to anyone from this most holy site.

Bulla from the sifting project bearing the partial name of someone identified as "son of Immer"

In order to secure the opportunity to sift the dirt, Israeli archaeologists' first task was moving the thousands of tons of earth from the Kidron Valley to the nearby Tzurim Valley National Park. A mechanical screener sifted the soil to minimize the amount of sifting done by hand. Then the dirt was manually resifted, a process that included washing the material and scrutinizing it to identify artifacts.

Common finds from the sifting project

Coin of Ptolemy III Euergetes from the sifting project

The soil has produced undeniable proof of a Jewish presence on the Temple Mount. From the First Temple period (approximately 971–586 BC), there was found Judean pottery, figurines, stone weights, seals, and even a Babylonian arrowhead dating from the destruction of Jerusalem in 586 BC. From the Second Temple period (approximately 516 BC–AD 70), archaeologists found pottery, architectural remains such as pieces of a capital, a dozen pieces of tile that once lined the Second Temple floor built by Herod the Great, hundreds of coins, and weapons, as well as other items.

Contrary to the ever-increasing propaganda regarding this site, the Temple Mount Sifting Project has proved there's an incontrovertible connection to Hebrew history and an overwhelming indication a Jewish temple existed on this place. Almost every single bucket that's sifted affirms Jewish history. The temples were once there, and there's archaeological proof to establish that.

34 NEBUCHADNEZZAR'S MADNESS
Archaeological and Medical Clues

The observation of a unique medical condition and the discovery of a related archaeological object could help explain one of the most bizarre accounts in the Bible—the divine punishment of the mighty king of Babylon Nebuchadnezzar.

According to the Bible, after the destruction of Jerusalem in 586 BC and at the zenith of his power, Nebuchadnezzar's heart was lifted up with pride (Daniel 4:28-30). The God of Israel then took away his royal authority by driving him from human society (Daniel 4:32). The most powerful king in the world was condemned to spend seven years in the fields with the wild animals and eat grass like an ox until he learned that the God of Israel has power over human kingdoms and can give them to anyone He chooses.

The medical term for Nebuchadnezzar's probable form of insanity is boanthropy (ox-man). In 1946, Dr. Raymond Harrison of England recorded a modern-day case of boanthropy. Dr. Harrison observed that the patient's only physical abnormalities were the lengthening of his hair and a thickened condition of the nails, the same anomalies that beset Nebuchadnezzar (Daniel 4:33). Also like the famous king's wanderings, the patient roamed the asylum

Nebuchadnezzar, William Blake

grounds from dusk till dawn eating handfuls of grass and drinking out of puddles like an animal.

Daniel 4:34-36 records that at the end of seven years, Nebuchadnezzar's faculties were fully restored, and he praised the God of Israel. There may be an archaeological clue to this period of Nebuchadnezzar's madness, which perhaps took place between 582 and 575 BC. Archaeologists haven't discovered any royal decrees by Nebuchadnezzar during this period, and the Babylonian army apparently didn't partake in military campaigns, presumably because of their king's incapacity.

As for the archaeological object linked to this narrative, Assyriologist A. K. Grayson published a sixth-century BC cuneiform tablet found in Babylon. Now on display at the British Museum, it states that Nebuchadnezzar's life appeared of no value. He continually gave contradictory orders and couldn't recognize his own family members or contribute in any of his building projects. This period of madness likely took place during the seven years he was driven from human society.

Through the data supplied by medical and archaeological research, we're able to measure the Bible's historical accuracy. In every instance where the Bible's claims can be tested, even in such bizarre narratives as the humbling of Nebuchadnezzar, the biblical account proves to be reliable.

Name: Babylonian Chronicle
Origin and date: Babylon 6th c. BC
Discovered: Babylon 19th c. AD
Size: width 2.44 inches, height 3.25 inches
Present location: British Museum

Babylonian Chronicle cuneiform tablet

35 NABONIDUS CYLINDER

Belshazzar and the Writing on the Wall

English archaeologists have unearthed treasures related to Belshazzar, the crown prince of Babylon, who literally saw the handwriting on the wall.

After the death of Nebuchadnezzar, the subsequent Babylonian rulers were Evil-Merodach (562–560 BC), Neriglissar (560–556 BC), Labashi Marduk (556 BC), Nabonidus (556–539 BC), and finally Belshazzar (553–539 BC). Belshazzar was considered a crown prince because he was left in control of the Babylonian kingdom while his father, Nabonidus, was on a hiatus in Arabia after conducting a military campaign there.

On the fateful night in approximately 539 BC when the short-lived Neo-Babylonian Empire was overthrown by the Medes, a miracle happened. Belshazzar held a great feast, during which his guests drank from the gold and silver vessels taken from the Jerusalem temple "and praised the gods of gold, and of silver, of brass, of iron, of wood, and of stone" (Daniel 5:1-4). Then the drunken crown prince saw the fingers of a hand write a cryptic message on the plaster wall of the king's palace (Daniel 5:5).

Unable to read it, Belshazzar was troubled and called for his wise men. When they couldn't tell him what it said, the queen recommended Daniel. He came and told Belshazzar that God had condemned his prideful heart, desecration of the temple vessels, and worship of false gods, saying his kingdom would be given to the Medes and Persians (Daniel 5:22-28).

The writing took place opposite a lampstand that illuminated it. It's possible this lampstand was the same one Nebuchadnezzar had taken from the temple in Jerusalem about 50 years earlier. Archaeologists have found a throne room in the palace of the Babylonian kings that was 56

Belshazzar's Feast, Rembrandt

feet wide and 173 feet long. It had plastered walls and was possibly the setting for this famous scene.

Three archaeological objects have confirmed that Belshazzar really did exist. These objects are on display at the British Museum. In 1854, British archaeologists explored the ruins of Ur in southern Iraq. While excavating an ancient tower, or ziggurat, built of mudbrick, they found several tiny cylinders buried in the brickwork. Each one measures about four inches long with lines of script. Once deciphered, the Nabonidus Cylinder (object 91125) turned out to be a prayer by King Nabonidus for favor with the gods. He mentions his eldest son Belshazzar as the heir apparent.

Later in 1882, Professor Theophilus Pinches published the Nabonidus Chronicle (object 35382), a tablet that mentions Belshazzar and places him as an equal to his father as a Babylonian official. In 1924, Sidney Smith of the British Museum published the investigation of the Persian Verse Account of Nabonidus

(object 38299), a tablet stating that Nabonidus entrusted the kingship to Belshazzar.

Once again, archaeology demonstrates the reliability and historical accuracy of the biblical record.

Nabonidus Chronicle

Name: Nabonidus Cylinder
Origin and date: 556–539 BC
Discovered: Austen Henry Layard et al
Size: length 4 inches, diameter 2 inches
Present location: British Museum

Nabonidus Cylinder

36 JEHOIACHIN RATION TABLET

Archaeological evidence found near the famous Ishtar Gate in the ancient city of Babylon corroborates the biblical account of Jehoiachin, who reigned as king of Judah for only three months before Nebuchadnezzar deposed him in 597 BC and replaced him with his uncle Mattaniah, whom Nebuchadnezzar renamed Zedekiah (2 Kings 24:17). Despite being carried off into captivity as a prisoner of war, Jehoiachin was spoken to kindly by Babylonian King Evil-Merodach, Nebuchadnezzar's grandson. The Bible says he gave Jehoiachin a higher place than all the other kings exiled to Babylon (2 Kings 25:27-30).

Administrative tablets were found by German archaeologist Robert Koldewey during excavations from 1899 to 1917 in a royal archive room of Nebuchadnezzar and his successors in Babylon. The storeroom produced many interesting finds, but none are as important to biblical archaeologists as the tablets that date to shortly after the destruction of Solomon's Temple in 586 BC. They contain an official government receipt of the deliveries of oil to different royal households held in exile by the Babylonians. One fragmented tablet mentions groceries delivered to none other than "Jehoiachin, king of Judah" and to the "sons of the king of Judah." The Jehoiachin ration tablet, now on display at the Pergamon Museum in Berlin, dates to just five years after he was taken captive.

This extrabiblical evidence mentioning the exact name of the next-to-last descendant of David to rule from the throne in Jerusalem is another notch in the belt for biblical archaeologists who seek to demonstrate the reliability and historical accuracy of the Bible. Jehoiachin really did exist, and he's one of over 100 people mentioned in the Bible whose names archaeologists have found on historical objects.

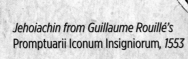

Jehoiachin from Guillaume Rouillé's Promptuarii Iconum Insigniorum, *1553*

Name: Jehoiachin ration tablet
Origin and date: Babylon ~592 BC
Discovered: Robert Koldewey 1899–1917
Size: width 4.1 inches, height 3.6 inches
Present location: Pergamon Museum, Berlin

Jehoiachin ration tablet

37 CYRUS CYLINDER

After being buried for almost 2,500 years, a remarkable object was discovered in 1879 by English archaeologists in Babylon. Just nine inches long, the Cyrus Cylinder records a decree given by King Cyrus of Persia that parallels his edict mentioned in Ezra 1:1-4. The cuneiform inscription on the cylinder states that Cyrus allowed groups of people to return to their homelands to rebuild their holy cities.

According to first-century AD Jewish historian Josephus, Cyrus the Great was aware that he had been marked out around 200 years earlier by the prophet Isaiah to rule in Israel's favor (*Antiquities* 11.1.1-2). To demonstrate the precision of Scripture, in the eighth century BC Isaiah

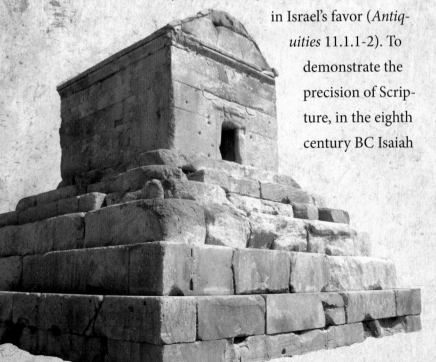

called Cyrus by name through the revelation of God. Isaiah called him God's "anointed" (Isaiah 45:1). This perhaps prompted the obedience of the superstitious Cyrus when he came to power in the sixth century BC.

When Cyrus appeared on the scene, there was no misunderstanding by the Jews or by Cyrus himself that he would be the man who would carry out the will of God. Cyrus decreed that the people of Israel could return to their land after their 70-year captivity in Babylon to build the God of Israel a temple in Jerusalem. Perhaps this was perceived as a recompense on behalf of Cyrus to honor the God of Israel for giving him all the kingdoms of the earth (Ezra 1:2). Cyrus didn't inherit the land. Instead, he earned it through years of military campaigns. This huge territory would have included India to the east; the Caspian and Black Seas to the north; Egypt, Turkey, and even into Greece to the west; Ethiopia to the south; and everything in between.

Although Cyrus' proclamation invited every Israelite from every tribe in the diaspora to go to Judah to rebuild the temple (Ezra 1:3), a great portion of the nation of

Tomb of Cyrus in Pasargadae, Iran

Israel in Babylonian captivity remained by preference in Babylonia, where they were prospering administratively, politically, religiously, and economically. Those who did go were successful in rebuilding the temple.

The correlation of the edict as recorded in the Bible and the one inscribed on the Cyrus Cylinder demonstrates that this archaeological object is directly related to the Bible's account of this event.

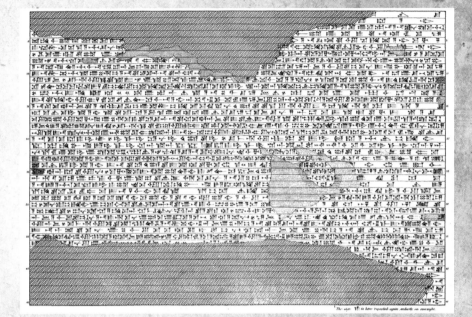

Name: Cyrus Cylinder
Origin and date: Babylon ~539 BC
Discovered: Hormuzd Rassom 1879
Size: length 8.6 inches, diameter ~4 inches
Present location: British Museum

EARLY CHURCH PERIOD

38 HEROD'S NAME AT MASADA

Archaeologists have found the first-ever inscription bearing the full title of the most infamous king in the New Testament—Herod the Great.

Ehud Netzer, who discovered Herod's tomb at the Herodium, found the inscription with the king's name at Masada, an isolated rock plateau that's about 1,300 feet high on its eastern side. It's surrounded on every side by very steep inclines, giving it the shape of a ship, with the plateau functioning as the deck. Masada is a naturally defensible location on the eastern edge of the Judean wilderness near the western shore of the Dead Sea. It's known for the Roman siege from AD 72 to 73 against Jewish holdouts there after the fall of Jerusalem in the First Jewish-Roman War.

Herod was well aware of the strategic advantages of controlling Masada. He chose the site as one of his strongholds and, according to Jewish historian Josephus, as the location for two palaces. During Herod's reign around 35 BC, luxurious structures were built on the plateau, in addition to storerooms, a synagogue, massive cisterns, and a casemate wall around the plateau's perimeter.

In 1996, Netzer and his team found a cave near the synagogue that appears to have been used as an ancient garbage dump. While cleaning out 2,000 years' worth of rubble, Netzer discovered numerous large, broken storage vessels known as amphorae and a variety of artifacts. These included food remains such as the shells and pits of nuts, eggs, dates, and olives, all of which were preserved due to the extremely dry climate in the region. The remains were likely trash generated by the crew of around 100 people who guarded the king's fortress.

Inscribed in Latin on one of the broken amphora pieces is the name and title "Herod, King of Judea." The

Name: Amphora fragment with Herod's name
Origin and date: Italy/Masada 19 BC
Discovered: Ehud Netzer 1996
Size: width four inches, height 2 inches
Present location: Israel Museum

Amphora

cone-shaped, two-handled jug upon which the inscription was found originally held around 20 gallons of wine and dates to about 19 BC. The wine was likely exported to the Holy Land from Italy.

This discovery related to Herod the Great testifies to the reliability and historical accuracy of the Bible. Herod was a real person who, as the gospels spell out, was the ruler of Judea who ordered the massacre of the innocents in a futile attempt to eliminate his rival, Jesus, the King of the Jews (Matthew 2:16).

Masada

39 HEROD'S TOMB

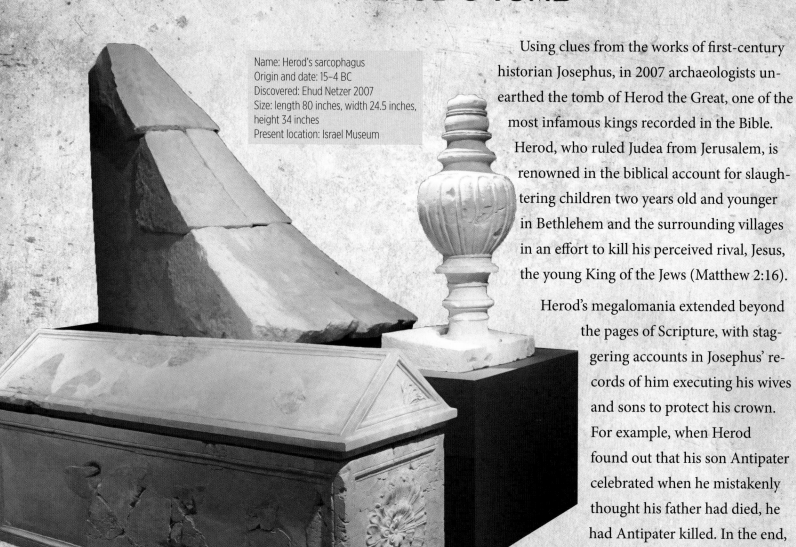

Name: Herod's sarcophagus
Origin and date: 15–4 BC
Discovered: Ehud Netzer 2007
Size: length 80 inches, width 24.5 inches, height 34 inches
Present location: Israel Museum

Using clues from the works of first-century historian Josephus, in 2007 archaeologists unearthed the tomb of Herod the Great, one of the most infamous kings recorded in the Bible. Herod, who ruled Judea from Jerusalem, is renowned in the biblical account for slaughtering children two years old and younger in Bethlehem and the surrounding villages in an effort to kill his perceived rival, Jesus, the young King of the Jews (Matthew 2:16).

Herod's megalomania extended beyond the pages of Scripture, with staggering accounts in Josephus' records of him executing his wives and sons to protect his crown. For example, when Herod found out that his son Antipater celebrated when he mistakenly thought his father had died, he had Antipater killed. In the end, the cruel king got what he de-

Herod's sarcophagus (front)

served and died a miserable death. According to Josephus, "his intestines…and colon were inflamed…his feet swelled and his loins were putrefied, producing worms" (*Antiquities* 17.6.5). He likely had inoperable liver or kidney cancer, complicated by some form of gangrene.

Josephus wrote that when Herod knew he was going to die, he planned to arrest and execute the principal Jewish leaders in Israel to ensure that the nation would mourn at the time of his death (*Antiquities* 17.6.5). For whom the Jews mourned didn't trouble Herod. Fortunately, after his death his sister, Salome, and her husband, Alexas, didn't carry out the order.

Herod's grand funeral procession, as recorded by Josephus, traveled from Jericho to his tomb at the Herodium, a fortress Herod built on the seam between the desert and farmland about three miles southeast of Bethlehem (*Antiquities* 17.8.3). The Herodium not only functioned as a palace for Herod but served to protect Jerusalem's interests from the southeast.

In 1972, Israeli archaeologist Ehud Netzer began excavations at the palace complex at the Herodium. He finally discovered Herod's mausoleum in 2007. Inside the 30 by 30-foot mausoleum with 80-foot-high ceilings, Netzer

Coins from the time of Herod the Great

found the king's sarcophagus, as well as the likely sarcophagi of his royal family members.

But someone had long ago beaten Netzer to the tomb. The bodies of Herod and the royal family were not found, and Herod's sarcophagus was greatly damaged. This suggests that someone discovered the tomb, smashed it, and destroyed the body, perhaps out of spite for this hated king, who his detractors claimed had collaborated with their enemy, Rome. This was perhaps done by Jewish rebels who protested against Rome in the Jewish revolts and used the impregnable Herodium as a hideout.

Thankfully, enough of the mausoleum was left intact to piece Herod's tomb back together. Pilgrims can visit the Israel Museum to see the actual sarcophagus and view this piece of archaeological evidence demonstrating the historical reliability of the Bible.

40 THE JESUS BOAT

Because of a record drought in Israel in 1985 and 1986, the waters of the Sea of Galilee receded. Two brothers who were amateur archaeologists and residents of Kibbutz Ginosar, which is located on the lake's western shore, explored the newly exposed lakebed. While searching for artifacts like anchors and coins that might have been uncovered by the drought, they stumbled upon an impressive sight—the faint outline of a boat buried in the mud.

Knowing that time was against them because rain was in the forecast, the community quickly gathered their resources. They planned to excavate the boat, study it as much as they could in situ, and then finally move it to the Yigal Allon Museum at Kibbutz Ginosar, just 550 yards away.

Once they started excavating, their suspicions were confirmed that the wood's structure was mainly supported by its immersion in water, and any evaporation would lead to its destruction. So, the boat was shaded from sunlight during the day. As soon as parts were exposed from the mud, they were covered with wet sponges and sprayed with water until the excavation was completed. The boat was also guarded night and day.

The team encased the entire boat in polyurethane to protect it while they floated it to the nearby museum. There, they constructed a conservation tank to store the boat until they could remove the polyurethane encasement and treat the boat so it could be displayed. Pieces of ancient pottery were discovered inside and near the boat, including an oil lamp and a cooking pot.

Sea of Galilee

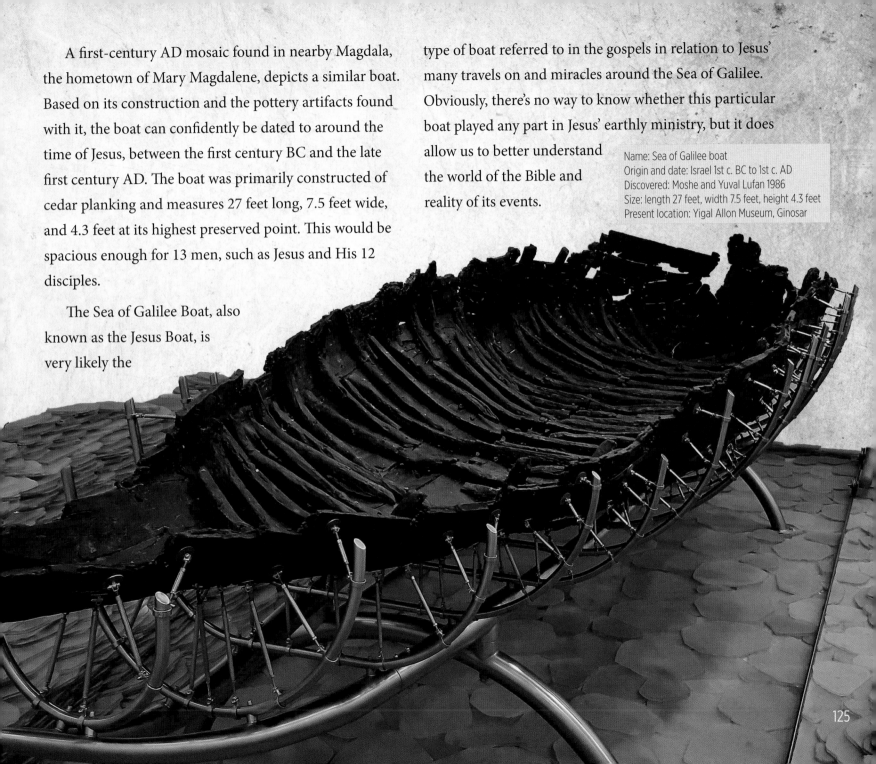

A first-century AD mosaic found in nearby Magdala, the hometown of Mary Magdalene, depicts a similar boat. Based on its construction and the pottery artifacts found with it, the boat can confidently be dated to around the time of Jesus, between the first century BC and the late first century AD. The boat was primarily constructed of cedar planking and measures 27 feet long, 7.5 feet wide, and 4.3 feet at its highest preserved point. This would be spacious enough for 13 men, such as Jesus and His 12 disciples.

The Sea of Galilee Boat, also known as the Jesus Boat, is very likely the type of boat referred to in the gospels in relation to Jesus' many travels on and miracles around the Sea of Galilee. Obviously, there's no way to know whether this particular boat played any part in Jesus' earthly ministry, but it does allow us to better understand the world of the Bible and reality of its events.

Name: Sea of Galilee boat
Origin and date: Israel 1st c. BC to 1st c. AD
Discovered: Moshe and Yuval Lufan 1986
Size: length 27 feet, width 7.5 feet, height 4.3 feet
Present location: Yigal Allon Museum, Ginosar

125

41 CAIAPHAS AND PONTIUS PILATE

Archaeological evidence has affirmed the existence of two of the main players in the accusation, trial, and death of Jesus—Caiaphas, the Jewish high priest, and Pontius Pilate, the governor of the Roman province of Judea.

Caiaphas was the leader of the Jewish Sanhedrin from AD 18 to 36 and, according to the gospel of John, advised the other Jewish leaders that it was expedient that one man, Jesus, should perish rather than the whole nation of Israel (John 11:50). The human remains and ossuary, or "bone box," of the Jewish high priest who plotted Jesus' death were discovered by chance. During the Second Temple period, an ossuary was a small stone chest used for the secondary burial of a deceased person's bones. It frequently had an inscription identifying the person inside.

In 1990, workers on a public works project south of the Old City of Jerusalem came across 12 limestone ossuaries when the roof of a burial chamber collapsed due to the construction. One ornate ossuary evidently belonged to a wealthy individual. The name etched on the limestone box read in one spot "Qafa" (Caiaphas) and in another "Yehosef bar Qayafa" (Joseph, son of Caiaphas). The New

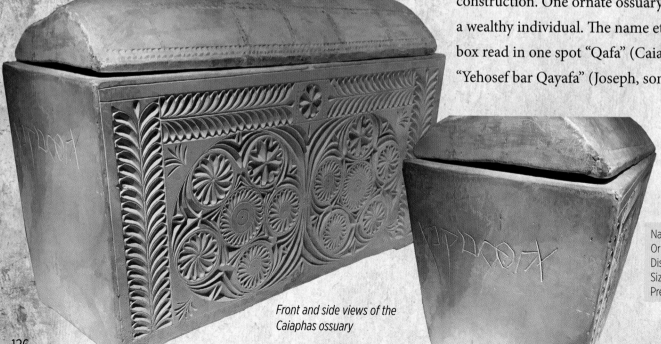

Front and side views of the Caiaphas ossuary

Name: Caiaphas ossuary
Origin and date: Jerusalem 1st c. AD
Discovered: 1990
Size: length 29.5 inches, height 14.6 inches
Present location: Israel Museum

Testament only refers to the Jewish high priest at the time of Jesus as Caiaphas, but the first-century Jewish historian Josephus identifies him as "Joseph who was called Caiaphas of the high priesthood" (*Antiquities* 18.4.3).

Regarding evidence for Pontius Pilate, Italian archaeologists in 1961 were excavating an ancient theater at Caesarea Maritima on the Mediterranean coast of Israel when they stumbled upon a first-century AD stone that had been reused in a fourth-century AD building. The archaeologists discovered that the stone slab was a plaque written to commemorate Pontius Pilate's donation of a temple dedicated to Tiberias Caesar, the Roman emperor of Judea at the time. Though the plaque is greatly damaged, it undeniably states in Latin "Pontius Pilate, Prefect of Judea." It is the only known record that is contemporary with his lifetime.

The archaeological discoveries related to Caiaphas and Pontius Pilate are another testimony to the reliability and historical accuracy of the Bible.

Name: Pilate stone
Origin and date: Caesarea Maritima AD 26–36
Discovered: 1961
Size: width 25.6 inches, height 32 inches
Present location: Israel Museum

42 Church of the Holy Sepulchre

Where was Calvary located?

Roman Emperor Hadrian, who ruled approximately AD 117 to 138, visited Jerusalem around AD 130, some 60 years after Roman Commander (later Emperor) Titus destroyed the city and the Jewish temple. In an effort to erase the memory of Jesus Christ, whom Hadrian saw as a threat to the Roman way of life, Hadrian built a temple honoring the Roman goddess Venus over the place where Jesus was reportedly crucified—the site of the present-day Church of the Holy Sepulchre. Hadrian also tried to do the same in Bethlehem by building a temple honoring the Roman god Adonis over the cave where Jesus was said to have been born and where the Church of the Nativity now stands.

However, the memory of Calvary's location lived on despite Rome's best efforts. In AD 324, Roman Emperor Constantine became the first Christian emperor to rule over the Holy Land. Constantine's mother, Helena, is credited with major building projects related to the life of Jesus. She had churches built over the sites of Jesus' birth in Bethlehem and crucifixion and resurrection in Jerusalem, the same places Hadrian had desecrated some 200 years earlier.

Consecrated in AD 335, the Church of the Holy Sepulchre was destroyed by fire during an invasion in AD 614 and was partly rebuilt. It was damaged and repaired several times until the Crusader period. The church we see today was constructed in the 12th century AD on top of Helena's fourth-century AD church, which had been built over the rock of Golgotha where Christ was crucified and the tomb where He was buried before His resurrection.

More than 2,000 years later, despite man's best efforts to destroy His memory, Jesus Christ continues to be the focus of the human race, and the Church of the Holy Sepulchre commemorates His passion. All the armies that ever marched, all the politicians who have ever legislated, all the leaders who have ever ruled put together haven't come close to impacting life on this earth as powerfully as one man, the resurrected Jesus Christ.

43 Calvary Pilgrim Inscription

An ancient inscription concealed for 1,700 years in the Church of the Holy Sepulchre points to the likely place where Jesus Christ was crucified.

In 1975, Dr. Magen Broshi, a leading Israeli archaeologist and Dead Sea Scrolls expert, was given the rare opportunity to lead excavation work at the eastern extremity of the Church of the Holy Sepulchre, which was built over the traditional location of Jesus' crucifixion and resurrection. A drawing on a stone had been noticed there in 1971, but Dr. Broshi was the first to really examine it. The image and its accompanying inscription have underlined the likelihood that this church is indeed situated at the actual place of Jesus' crucifixion.

The drawing is of a small Roman sailing ship dating to the very beginning of the Byzantine Empire, around AD 330. The date is determined by the type of ship, the inscription, and the layer in which the find was made. In AD 335, construction of the Church of the Holy Sepulchre was completed. The church had been commissioned by the mother of Roman Emperor Constantine, Helena, who demolished the pagan shrine Roman Emperor Hadrian had built in approximately AD 132–136 over the original reported site of Jesus' crucifixion. The ship inscription had to be made before AD 335, because the area Dr. Broshi excavated had been filled in and made inaccessible due to the church's construction.

The drawing, which includes the Latin inscription DOMINE IVIMUS, or "Lord, we went," was found on a smooth stone about 33 inches long by 18 inches high and fixed in a wall of rougher stones. The inscription was likely made by pilgrims who came from the western part of the Roman Empire to visit Jerusalem. Romans in the west used Latin, whereas Romans in the east used Greek. Their pilgrimage was likely for the purpose of visiting the empty tomb of the Lord, hence the stone's message. But the inscription is also an allusion to Psalm 122:1, which says in Latin *In domum Domini ibimus*, or "Let us go into the house of the Lord."

From this small site, the stones themselves cry out that this is the place where early pilgrims came to worship their resurrected Savior, Jesus Christ.

Name: Jerusalem ship drawing
Origin and date: Jerusalem ~AD 330
Discovered: 1971
Size: Ship drawing length 26 inches, height 12.2 inches
Present location: Church of the Holy Sepulchre, Jerusalem

44　TRUMPETING PLACE INSCRIPTION

Charles Warren, a British Royal Engineer who was also a real-life Indiana Jones, is credited with conducting the first major archaeological excavations at the Temple Mount in Jerusalem. While digging an excavation shaft at the base of the mount's southwest corner in the late 19th century, Warren penetrated the first-century pavement laid by Herod the Great and perhaps cracked the edge of a large stone that had been buried there for almost 2,000 years.

This stone, now called the Trumpeting Place inscription, wasn't discovered by Warren at that time. It remained hidden for about 100 more years until it was found in 1968 by Israeli archaeologist Benjamin Mazar. It's possible the stone broke when it was thrown off the top of the Temple Mount by the Romans in AD 70, thus fulfilling the prophecy of Jesus that the temple would be completely demolished and "there shall not be left here one stone upon

Name: Trumpeting Place inscription
Origin and date: Jerusalem 1st c. BC
Discovered: Benjamin Mazar 1968
Size: length 33 inches. width 10 inches
height 12 inches
Present location: Israel Museum

another, that shall not be thrown down" (Matthew 24:2).

However it was broken, this stone is unlike the others the Romans threw down when they destroyed the temple—it bears a Hebrew inscription. Because the inscription is incomplete, its interpretation is uncertain, although it likely says "to the place of trumpeting…" This discovery confirms the testimony of Josephus, the first-century Jewish historian, who stated that the Jewish priests had a designated place to stand on the Temple Mount from which to sound a shofar, or trumpet, marking the beginning and ending of the Sabbath (*Of the War* 4.9.12). The blowing of the trumpet was also used for other religious and military occasions.

The Trumpeting Place inscription is now on display at the Israel Museum in Jerusalem.

Trumpeting Place reconstruction in Jerusalem

133

45 DEAD SEA SCROLLS

The site of Qumran near the northwestern shore of the Dead Sea draws visitors from all over the world. It is best known for one of the most significant manuscript discoveries ever made—the Dead Sea Scrolls.

Many people have heard of this discovery in the winter of 1946–1947 by a young Bedouin shepherd. According to one tale, he was searching for a stray when a cave on a steep rocky hillside caught his eye. He threw a stone into it and, hearing breaking pottery, climbed up to discover large clay jars. Most were empty, but two contained ancient scrolls. When word spread, more scrolls were found in nearby caves.

According to Dr. Randall Price in *The Stones Cry Out*, the Dead Sea Scrolls represent over 1,000 ancient documents.[4] They consist of numerous intact scrolls, plus over 100,000 fragments that date to before and after the time of Jesus, third century BC to first entury AD. About 23% of the total manuscripts are copies of Old Testament writings. The entirety or a portion of every Old Testament book has been found in the Dead Sea Scroll library, except for the book of Esther.

Today the collection of biblical texts in the Dead Sea

Scrolls constitutes our oldest known copies of the Bible. Other types of texts such as the Copper Scroll are also a part of the Dead Sea Scroll library. Among other things, the scrolls demonstrate how accurately the Jewish scribes transmitted the Old Testament. Prior to the 1946–1947 discovery of the scrolls, the oldest known complete version of the Old Testament was the Aleppo Codex (~AD 935). According to Dr. Price, when the two texts were compared, it was revealed, amazingly, that they are almost identical.

The Israel Antiquities Authority returned to the region following reports that locals were scavenging the caves in the Judean wilderness for priceless ancient scrolls. Consequently, Israeli archaeologists recently found more biblical scrolls dated to around AD 135 in the Cave of Horror in Nahal Hever, some 25 miles from Qumran. Archaeologists gave the cave this name because of the remains of Jewish refugees from the Bar Kokhba Revolt (AD 132–135) discovered there.

With increasing discoveries made over the years, are there more to come? Could it be that we are on the verge of yet another great discovery of ancient scrolls?

Qumran Cave 4 has produced the majority of the Dead Sea Scrolls

Name: Dead Sea Scrolls
Origin and date: 3rd c. BC to 1st c. AD
Discovered: ~1946 onward
Size: varied
Present location: Israel Museum

46 ISAIAH SCROLL

When the first Dead Sea Scrolls were discovered by a young Bedouin shepherd, he and his companions sold them to antiquities dealers. Four of the scrolls found their way into the hands of Mar Samuel, head of the Syrian Orthodox Church in Jerusalem. One of them turned out to be the oldest known complete manuscript of the biblical book of Isaiah.

The scroll, which is now in Jerusalem's Shrine of the Book Museum, measures 24 feet long by up to 10.6 inches high. It's made of 17 leather sheets sewn end to end

Name: Isaiah scroll
Origin and date: 1st c. BC
Discovered: Bedouin shepherd ~1946
Size: length 24 feet, height 10 to 10.6 inches
Present location: Israel Museum

and consists of 54 columns of Hebrew writing. Before the discovery of the Isaiah Scroll, which dates to shortly before the time of Jesus Christ, about 100–150 BC, the oldest known copy of Isaiah dated to around AD 1000.

When the Isaiah Scroll is compared to its counterpart in the Aleppo Codex, there's little to no difference; they are virtually the same. The few textual variants that exist aren't theological but grammatical in nature. It's evident by comparing these documents from over 1,000 years apart that the Jewish scribes took great care to faithfully transmit the biblical record.

As archaeology has demonstrated, the Hebrew Bible, on which modern translations of the Old Testament are based, hasn't changed. God really has preserved His Word.

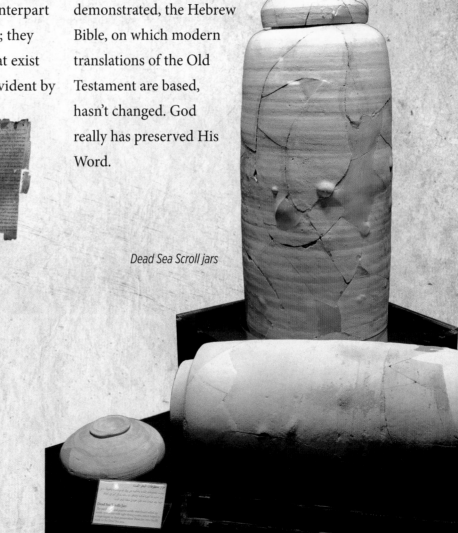

Dead Sea Scroll jars

137

47 THE COPPER SCROLL

A Treasure Waiting to Be Found

In the spring of 1952, an unexpected discovery was made in Qumran Cave 3 near the location where the original Dead Sea Scrolls were found—two separated sections of a single manuscript made from sheets of almost pure copper that are engraved with Hebrew text.

View of the Dead Sea from a Qumran cave

The Copper Scroll details in cryptic language the resting places of a great treasure yet to be discovered. According to the scroll, there are massive amounts of gold coins, solid gold bars, vessels full of silver coins, and sacred vessels made of pure silver and gold that are consecrated to the worship of the Hebrew God. Just the gold coins, whose measure is given in talents, would be worth billions of dollars. These treasures of biblical proportions are quite possibly the riches of the Jewish temple hidden by the Israelites shortly before the Romans destroyed their capital city of Jerusalem and their temple in AD 70.

When the Copper Scroll was first found, experts were uncertain how to open the brittle oxidized scroll. They discussed various ways, and finally in 1956 the scroll was sawn into segments at Manchester College of Technology in England. It was discovered that the scroll is written in Mishnaic, or postbiblical Hebrew. This treasure map, which is currently on display at the Jordan Museum in Amman, lists around 60 different places where the enormous treasure was hidden.

According to the scroll, the treasures are buried near Jerusalem and in hiding places around the Dead Sea and Jericho. The map gives often cryptic descriptions of the locations where the treasures are buried. Many of the places may no longer exist or would otherwise be unrecognizable after all this time. It also gives information about the area's topography, how far below the surface the treasure is buried, and the kind and amount of treasure buried in the spot. A sample excerpt from the map reads, "In the cistern which is below the rampart, on the east side, in a place hollowed out of the rock, there are 600 bars of silver."

The map evidently existed in part with the hope that a team of diggers would recover the temple treasure and its sacred vessels after the Jews successfully repelled the Roman invasion. But, of course, Rome overcame the Jews in AD 70, and the treasure—if it still exists—remains buried, ready to lure new adventure hunters.

Name: Copper Scroll
Origin and date: 1st c. AD
Discovered: Qumran 1952
Size: original length ~8 feet
Present location: Jordan Museum, Amman

The Oldest New Testament Text

On display at the John Rylands Library in Manchester, England, is the oldest known portion of the New Testament. The tiny fragment measuring 2.5 inches by 3.5 inches contains 114 Greek letters. There are parts of seven lines from John 18:31-33 on one side and parts of seven lines from John 18:37-38 on the other. Since the fragment has writing on both sides, it's clear it came from a sewn and folded book rather than a scroll.

This particular portion of John's gospel concerns Jesus' appearance before Pontius Pilate. The Rylands Library Papyrus 52, or P52, was acquired in Egypt in 1920 by English Egyptologist Bernard Grenfell. The translation of the text wasn't done until 1934 by the scholar Colin Roberts. The fragment was then dated to around AD 100–125.

Despite its small size, this papyrus fragment is extremely important. If the dating is correct, it attests that the gospel of John spread far from Ephesus in Asia Minor, where Christian tradition puts the original authorship of the book, and was being read in the Christian community of Egypt just after John's death, traditionally around 100 AD. The P52 fragment

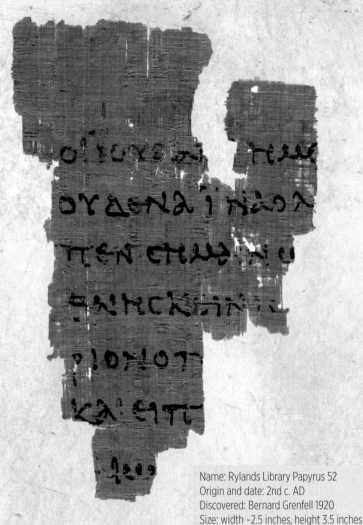

Name: Rylands Library Papyrus 52
Origin and date: 2nd c. AD
Discovered: Bernard Grenfell 1920
Size: width ~2.5 inches, height 3.5 inches
Present location: John Rylands Library, Manchester, England

undermines any attempt to put a very late date on John's gospel.

To demonstrate the uniqueness of the find, consider that in some Greek or Latin literature, the oldest known fragment dates to 1,000 years after the original autographs. Scholars estimate the writing of Homer's *The Odyssey* to be around 725–675 BC. In 2018, a tablet was found near the ruins of the Temple of Zeus with portions of *The Odyssey* written on it and dated to the early Byzantine period (around the third century AD), some 1,000 years after its original composition.

The discovery of the P52 fragment just a generation after the death of John is absolutely remarkable. An abundance of ancient Greek New Testament texts exists. Roughly 5,500 separate manuscripts are known, ranging from the entire New Testament to tiny fragments like P52. These manuscripts, even ones as small as P52, provide tremendous assurance to Christians around the world that their New Testament translations are based on texts that accurately reflect the original autographs from 2,000 years ago.

Indeed, Jesus Himself has promised that though the heavens and the earth will disappear, His words never will (Matthew 24:35).

John the Apostle, Pyotr Basin

141

49 MEGIDDO MOSAIC

A chance discovery revealed not only the oldest church ever found in the Holy Land but also the earliest archaeological example of Jesus Christ's written name.

In 2005, construction crews were putting an addition onto a modern-day maximum security prison near the pivotal site of Megiddo in Israel. They accidentally came across a significant find—the remains of an ancient church. It probably dates to the third century AD, some

Name: Megiddo mosaic
Origin and date: 3rd c. AD
Discovered: Yotam Tepper 2005
Present location: Megiddo, Israel

200 years after the death and resurrection of Christ and 100 years before Christianity became the official religion of the Byzantine Empire (AD 326–640).

It's quite possible that early Christians remodeled an existing Roman building at this key intersection and converted it into a church. One of the most significant discoveries there thus far is located within the large mosaic that decorated the church floor. The mosaic contains beautiful geometric designs and early Christian symbols such as fish. But the pièce de résistance is a Greek inscription honoring a Christian named Akeptous, who dedicated a religious table to be used in the honor of "God, Jesus Christ." Excluding manuscripts, this is the earliest archaeological discovery mentioning the name and divinity of Christ.

Because of this discovery's importance, the Israeli government stopped the expansion of the prison and covered up the church remains in order to preserve them. The government actually plans to relocate the entire maximum security prison to another location so more archaeological work can be done at the site. Some day pilgrims from around the world will be able to visit the earliest known Holy Land church.

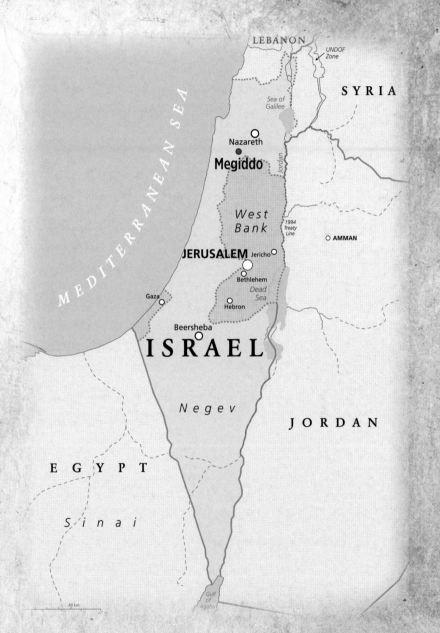

143

50 MADABA MAP
The Oldest Holy Land Map

An archaeological discovery in modern-day Jordan vividly demonstrates the historicity of many places mentioned in the Bible.

The floor of St. George's Church in Madaba, Jordan, features the remnants of a remarkable mosaic. Dating to the sixth century AD, it is the oldest and most exact known map of the Holy Land before modern cartography. Because of the discovery of this mosaic and several others in the area, Madaba is known as the City of Mosaics.

The map was created for a church in the early Byzantine period, probably during the reign of Emperor Justinian, who ruled approximately AD 527–565. The mosaic was rediscovered in 1884 when a Greek Orthodox church was built where the Byzantine church once stood. Research on the map, however, didn't begin until 1896. Over time, much of the map had been chipped away, damaged, or destroyed, but a large section remains. In 1965, a German archaeological team carried out a restoration of the mosaic.

The restored but incomplete map is huge, measuring around 35 feet across and 16 feet high. There were likely two million mosaic cubes or more needed for this project. The map is oriented to the east, corresponding to the orientation of many Byzantine churches of the time. The preserved fragments show numerous topographical features of the Holy Land like the Jordan River running into the Dead Sea, fountains and springs, the eastern mountains of Moab, the mountainous area of Ephraim and Manasseh north of Jerusalem, the lowlands or Shephelah, the coastal region, the biblical Negev, and parts of the Mediterranean Sea and the Nile Delta.

The map also represents the zoology and foliage of the Holy Land in the early Byzantine period. There are images of lions, gazelles, and fish, as well as plants such as date palms. Maritime activity is depicted on the Dead Sea, with ships transporting cargo.

Greek inscriptions portray Bible verses, as well as pinpoint where famous biblical events occurred. And of course, biblical towns and cities are located on the map, along with their corresponding names in Greek. Smaller towns, medium-size cities, and larger cities are shown with varying numbers of gates and/or towers. The centerpiece of the map is the enlarged city of Jerusalem, with such prominent locations as the Damascus Gate, the Cardo Maximus (main north-south street), the Nea Church, and the Church of the Holy Sepulchre.

The Madaba map is not only a piece of art history but a testimony to the historical veracity of the places and events recorded in the pages of the Bible.

Name: Madaba Map
Origin and date: 6th c. AD
Discovered: 1884
Size: width ~35 feet, height 16 feet
Present location: St. George's Church, Madaba, Jordan

CONCLUSION

Thank you for going on this adventure with me through the world of the Bible. We covered a lot of time—over 2,000 years of biblical history—and a lot of territory, from the southern pole of Egypt to the northern pole of Israel. And we just scratched the surface.

Our expedition together has accomplished what we set out to do, which is demonstrating that every time the Bible's claims can be tested, they stand up to scrutiny. The people and places mentioned in the Bible really did exist, and the events reported in Scripture really did happen exactly as they are described.

As I said at our journey's beginning, we don't need archaeology to convince us of the reliability and accuracy of Scripture. Jesus Christ Himself did that when He said, "[God's] word is truth" (John 17:17). But it's helpful to have such a tsunami of evidence that clearly validates the biblical account.

Having a knowledge that the Bible is true, however, without having a saving faith in Jesus Christ will not rescue you from the judgment to come. What will save you is believing "that Christ died for our sins according to the scriptures; and that he was buried, and that he rose again the third day according to the scriptures" (1 Corinthians 15:3-4).

In the end, this is what the truth of the Bible leads us to: "For God so loved the world, that he gave his only begotten Son, that whosoever believeth in him should not perish, but have everlasting life" (John 3:16). If you haven't yet placed your faith in the Son of God, I invite you to do so today.

REFERENCES

1. Davies, Philip R. 1994. "House of David" Built on Sand: The Sins of the Biblical Maximizers. *Biblical Archaeology Review*. 20 (4): 55.

2. Wilson, Charles W. 1886. *Ordnance Survey of Jerusalem*. Under the direction of Colonel Sir Henry James, R.E. F.R.S. &c. Director of the Ordnance Survey.

3. Price, Randall. 2003. *Fast Facts® on the Middle East Conflict*. Eugene, OR: Harvest House Publishers, 125.

4. Price, Randall. 1997. *The Stones Cry Out*. Eugene, OR: Harvest House Publishers.

IMAGE CREDITS

: top, b: bottom, l: left, m: middle, r: right)

na al'ain via Wikimedia: 108b

ruce Allardice via Wikimedia: 93r

sama Shukir Muhammed Amin FRCP (Glasg): 3br, 79r, 93l, 111, 115, 139

yacheslav Argenberg via Wikimedia: 59

eror Avi via Wikimedia: 33, 40t, 41, 97b

abelStone via Wikimedia: 92

igstock: 13, 17t, 22, 32, 38, 44-45, 49-50, 51b, 62, 4, 70r, 72, 75, 95tr, 100t, 102, 120, 134, 143, 144

ukvoed via Wikimedia: 24, 25t, 88-89

hrisO via Wikimedia: 113t

lassical Numismatic Group: 109l

achi Dvira via Wikimedia: 109r

keidar via Wikimedia: 133t

askah Eksekrasi via Wikimedia: 15

ric Gaba via Wikimedia Commons: 14b

ugganij via Wikimedia: 40b

m Haberman via Wikimedia: 57b

anay via Wikimedia: 23, 25b

amar Hayardeni via Wikimedia: 35, 91, 133b

gsoc via Wikimedia: 106bl, 123

Ismoon via Wikimedia 43l

iStockPhoto: 121b

Steven G. Johnson and Gary Todd via Wikimedia: 78-79b

Rob Koopman via Flickr: 12

Kurohito via Wikimedia: 19t

Clint Loveness: 29, 63, 66, 77tlr, 83, 86, 103, 122, 124, 126-127, 129, 135r

Davide Mauro via Wikimedia: 137r

Mbzt 2022 via Wikimedia: 74

Hosanna Meyer: 95br

M.Lubinski via Wikimedia: 21

MohmmadRjab via Wikimedia: 37

Mujaddara via Wikimedia: 30

Naunakhte via Wikimedia Commons: 14t

NebMaatRa via Wikimedia: 19b

Vladimir Neichin via Wikimedia: 108tl

Onceinawhile via Wikimedia: 54

Ori~ via Wikimedia: 56l

Persian Dutch Network via Wikimedia: 116

Prioryman via Wikimedia: 117b

Public domain: 10, 16-17b, 20, 26, 28, 31, 36, 42, 43tr, 48, 51t, 52, 55, 57t, 60, 68-69, 73, 76, 77b, 80, 81b, 82, 84bl, br, 90, 95l, 96tr, 98l, 104, 106tr, 110, 112, 114, 117t, 118, 121tr, 135l, 136-137l, 138, 140-141

Carole Raddato via Wikimedia: 145

Zev Radovan: 56t, 81t, 84tr, 94, 96bl, 97tr, 121tl

Ranbar via Wikimedia: 131

Rémih via Wikimedia: 58

Ian Scott via Wikimedia: 71, 87

Shadsluiter via Wikimedia: 100-101b

Andrew Shiva via Wikimedia: 67, 107

Olaf Tausch via Wikimedia: 18, 53

Gary Todd via Wikimedia: 70l, 113b

Lev Tsimbler via Wikimedia: 46-47

Vesafis Tzferris via Wikimedia: 142

Wellcome Images: 39, 85

Berthold Werner: 65

Wilson44691 via Wikimedia: 98r

Andrey Zeigarnik via Wikimedia: 132

Israel Zeller: 125

Zunkir via Wikimedia: 99

Index

ABOUT THE INSTITUTE FOR CREATION RESEARCH

At the Institute for Creation Research, we want you to know God's Word can be trusted with everything it speaks about—from how and why we were made, to how the universe was formed, to how we can know God and receive all He has planned for us.

That's why ICR scientists have spent more than 50 years researching scientific evidence that refutes evolutionary philosophy and confirms the Bible's account of a recent and special creation. We regularly receive testimonies from around the world about how ICR's cutting-edge work has impacted thousands of people with God's creation truth.

HOW CAN ICR HELP YOU?

You'll find faith-building science articles in *Acts & Facts*, our bimonthly science news magazine, and spiritual insight and encouragement from *Days of Praise*, our quarterly devotional booklet. Sign up for FREE at **ICR.org/subscriptions**.

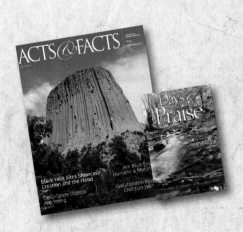

Our radio programs, podcasts, online videos, and wide range of social media offerings will keep you up to date on the latest creation news and announcements. Get connected at **ICR.org**.

We offer creation science books, DVDs, and other resources for every age and stage at **ICR.org/store**.

Learn how you can attend or host a biblical creation event at **ICR.org/events**.

Discover how science confirms the Bible at our Dallas museum, the ICR Discovery Center. Plan your visit at **ICRdiscoverycenter.org**.

ICR
INSTITUTE
FOR **CREATION**
RESEARCH

P. O. Box 59029
Dallas, TX 75229
800.337.0375
ICR.org

Proverbs

A Verse-by-Verse Guide to the Bible's Book of Wisdom

A word fitly spoken is like apples of gold in pictures of silver. (Proverbs 25:11)

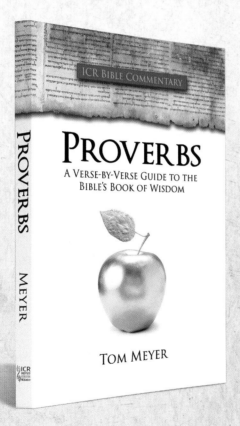

In *Proverbs: A Verse-by-Verse Guide to the Bible's Book of Wisdom*, Tom Meyer combines research, memorization, and his higher education in the land of the Bible to reveal fascinating explanations, insights, and cultural comments on the book of Proverbs.

Tom has an M.A. in the Historical Geography of Israel and an M.A. in Middle East Culture and Religion from Jerusalem University College. His unique perspectives on Proverbs seen through the lens of Middle Eastern culture, geography, archaeology, and customs will enrich your understanding of the Bible's book of wisdom.